A Funny
Thing Happened
on the Way
to Heaven!

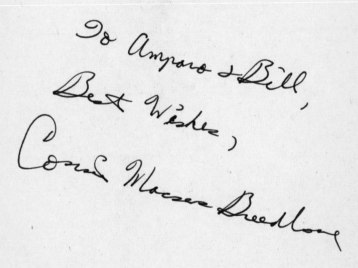

To Amparo & Bill,
Best Wishes,
Conn Mowser Breedlove

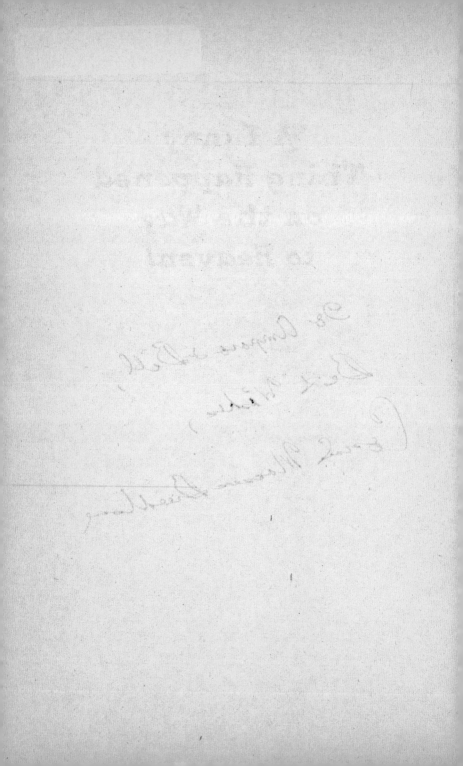

A Funny Thing Happened on the Way to Heaven!

CONNIE MACSAS BREEDLOVE

ZondervanPublishingHouse

Grand Rapids, Michigan

A Division of HarperCollinsPublishers

A Funny Thing Happened on the Way to Heaven
Copyright © 1996 by Connie Macsas Breedlove

Requests for information should be addressed to:

🏛 ZondervanPublishingHouse
Grand Rapids, Michigan 49530

Library of Congress Cataloging-in-Publication Data

Breedlove, Connie Macsas, 1939–
    A funny thing happened on the way to heaven / Connie Macsas
Breedlove.
        p.   cm.
    ISBN: 0-310-20909-9 (pbk.)
     1. Breedlove, Connie Macsas, 1939–   .   2. Christian biography—United
States.   3. Christian life—Humor.   I. Title.
BR1725.B6833A3   1996
209'.2—dc20
   [B]   96-16083
                                             CIP

Edited by Mary McNeil
Interior design by Sherri Hoffman

Printed in the United States of America

96 97 98 99 00 01 02 03 /❖ DH/ 10 9 8 7 6 5 4 3 2 1

To my husband, Len, who has supported my writing habit for twenty-six years and who has in this past year, when I've been busy with the book, cheerfully accepted peanut butter sandwiches for breakfast—even when the jelly jar was empty.

Contents

Acknowledgments   9

Introduction   11

1. A Sticky Situation   13
2. Ee-i-ee-i-Ouch!   19
3. We're in the Dough, Now   24
4. This Little Piggy Went to Day Care   29
5. Those Little-Town Blues   36
6. Thou Shalt Not Imply   39
7. We Really Got Her Goat   42
8. Redundancy Alert   45
9. Do You Think Anyone Noticed?   48
10. Hooray for the Fifth of July   51
11. Boo!   54
12. Just Hop on My Back   57
13. Don't Look Now . . .   62
14. Say What?   65
15. Sink or Swim   70
16. The Writing's on the Wall   73
17. Put My Best Foot Where?   78
18. Bottom Heavy   83
19. A Worm Is a Worm, and by Any Other Name . . .   88
20. So Where's the Fire?   94
21. A Hair-Raising Experience   100
22. What This Country Needs Is a Good,
    Five-Cent Car!   103

23. Oops! 107
24. Shhh! 111
25. Do You Feel a Draft? 118
26. I'll Take Chocolate 123
27. It's Knot Right! 128
28. I Didn't See That! 134
29. Whatcha Mean, Get Organized? 138
30. And Baby Makes Three 142
31. Car Wars 148
32. Whoa! 152
33. Tall in the Saddle . . . For a Few Minutes 158
34. Under—Way, Way Under—Construction 165

Acknowledgments

I've discovered that writing a book is the easy part, it's what takes place from the time the book is sold until it gets on the shelves in bookstores that tends to get a little hectic. I was moaning and groaning about some of it, and someone told me that if I pray for rain, I shouldn't gripe about the mud. So I stopped griping—most of the time— and all the time in front of my friends who are gracious enough to tell me to put a lid on it.

Since I did ask the Lord if He would mind blessing this book, I would like to acknowledge Him right from the start, because if He hadn't blessed it, there would be no need for any acknowledgments, anyhow.

I want to thank not only my parents, but all of my family, because they are all a big part of the tapestry that has been my experiences in life.

And a special thanks to Malvina for jumping into this without really knowing if there was water in the pool or not.

And thanks to Donna Abla, Judy Thompson, Susan Harmon, and Becky Hall for cheering me on when I needed cheering and for all of the good advice and encouragement given over some really good coffee.

And to Paul Guay, Dr. George Howe, Paul Walburg, and Pat Gundry for all their help and encouragement, without which this book would still be in my desk drawer instead of on the market.

And to Ed van der Maas and Mary McNeil for their invaluable help in the editing process.

And a very special thanks to Stan Gundry for his perseverance and encouragement in helping this first-time author achieve her dream.

And I want to thank my husband, Len, my son, Jim, and my daughter, Chris, for allowing me to make portions of their lives, literally, an open book. And thanks to Ben and Joy Lynn, who are also an intricate part of the family tapestry. And thanks to my daughter-in-law, Connie, for putting up with the confusion of living in the same town with me and sharing the same name—also for doing my Christmas shopping for me.

Introduction

I think God gave us a sense of humor because He knew we would need it—not only to deal with each other but with the telephone company as well.

He has seen to it that we receive generous helpings of joy on this trip. It seems that the simpler something is, the more joy we get out of it.

One summer several years back, we had a snow-cone stand. It was usually pretty busy, but sometimes there was time to just lean on the counter and wait for customers. This particular day I was enjoying some leaning time when I noticed a big snake crawling in front of the stand.

My first impulse was to call 911. As it turned out, it was just an old grass snake, so I told myself that unless he decided to come in for a snow-cone, I wouldn't push the panic button.

He didn't seem to be particularly interested in the flavor of the day, so I relaxed and watched him as he went on his way.

There was a creek about sixty yards from the stand, and that seemed to be where he was heading.

But as he passed by, there was a mud puddle off to one side that attracted his attention. He made his way over to the puddle and crawled in. He began turning over and over in that puddle. He was having a ball! I could almost hear him yelling, "Whoopee!"

Then he went on his way to the creek. It was just a quick side trip that he took on the way to his final destination. And he seemed to thoroughly enjoy it!

God has provided us with many side trips on our way to heaven. Enjoy them.

A Sticky Situation

I remember a summer during World War II when sugar was being rationed. That was long before anyone came up with the idea for sugar-free gum, so that meant there was a severe shortage of bubble gum. I was around eight or nine at the time, and a bubble-gum shortage was a serious thing.

There was an abundance of things to be bought for a penny, but bubble gum was the *elite* of the penny products. In fact, if you had a nickel, you might just buy five pieces of bubble gum instead of a more expensive nickel item. When bubble gum was no longer available, it was really hard for millions of bubble-gum-addicted kids to cope.

We managed to find ways to compensate, although some of them were more of an endurance test than a compensation.

There were about a dozen kids on our block, some of them tougher than others, but one little boy, James, was really tough. Being a girl, I didn't have to keep proving to the world that I was so tough, but the boys on the block didn't have it so easy. They were continually having to try and save face with James.

So the day they saw him digging hot tar out of the cracks of the sidewalk and chewing it, they had no choice but to follow suit. As bad as it tasted, not a one of them wanted to admit that chewing tar wasn't the most natural, manly thing in the world to do.

When I came ambling along and saw all of them chewing tar as if it tasted good, I just had to try some. It tasted awful. *Really* awful. I spit mine out, but the boys kept right on chewing. I had to admire them for that.

But from that day on, whenever any of the boys saw James digging tar out of the sidewalk, they suddenly heard their mothers calling . . .

Right in the middle of this big bubble-gum shortage, my uncle somehow managed to get a hold of a whole *box* of bubble gum. I remember the day he brought the box over. To us bubble-gum-starved kids it was like having Fort Knox sitting on our kitchen table, only better.

The gum wasn't all for me. I had to share it with my brother and sister. And not only did we have to share it, but we had to survive on a daily ration of one piece for each of us. And when my mother said "one piece a day," she meant *one piece a day*. If it got dropped, it got washed. If it got swallowed, too bad. We couldn't believe it—to be so close to pure ecstasy and to have it *rationed* out like a pair of nylons.

Just to be sure we weren't overpowered by temptation and didn't succumb to that most abominable sin— greeeed—my mother put the gum on the top shelf of the kitchen cabinet.

Then one day, when I wasn't looking, temptation and greed joined forces and jumped right in the middle of me.

It all started out innocently enough: Mother was next door having coffee, and my sister and I were outside playing. I came in for a drink of water. I had to stand on a chair to reach the first shelf, where the glasses were kept. As I stood there, I looked up and caught sight of Fort Knox sitting on the top shelf.

Well, being that close to that much bubble gum inspired me to reach for new heights. As I climbed higher for a closer look, I thought I could hear the Mormon Tabernacle Choir singing the "Hallelujah Chorus." Suddenly, that box of bubble gum became Mount Everest, and I had to climb up to it simply because it was *there!*

I climbed onto the top of the cabinet, holding onto the bottom shelf with one hand. I reached up and the next thing I knew, I was holding that awesome box of gum in my hand. The very smell of it made me giddy.

In my light-headed condition, I didn't hear my sister, Malvina, come in. I was just preparing to taste the fruits of my labor when her voice brought me back to reality, reminding me of the wages of sin. "Awwmmm, I'm telling Mama!" she said, bristling with righteous indignation.

Now, righteous indignation can be a delicious emotion if you're on the right end of it, and, believe me, she was savoring every second of it.

Fear, on the other hand, can be a very *useful* emotion. I had heard of people who had superhuman strength for a few seconds in life-threatening situations. And if there was ever a life-threatening situation for me, this was it. But it was my *mind* that had a surge of strength: It became sharper, more alert. I had a sudden burst of realization. In that split second, I knew what would taste better to her than righteous indignation.

"I'll give you a piece of gum if you don't tell," I said.

I watched her self-righteousness disappear like magic. I wasn't surprised—I knew I had her.

But she knew she had me, too.

"I want two pieces," she said.

"No! Mom will notice if that much is gone!"

"Then I'm telling," she said, sticking her lower lip out in a perfect Shirley Temple pout.

I knew then that the only thing more disgusting than a self-righteous five-year-old was a self-righteous extortionist.

My back was against the wall. My choices were limited to paying up or being turned over to the hanging judge.

I dropped the two pieces of extorted booty into her outstretched hand. She just stood there looking from the gum in her hand to the gum in the box, and I didn't like what I saw in her eyes.

"One more," she said.

"No!" I yelled, beginning to feel the effects of being bullied by a five-year-old.

She dropped the gum to the floor and headed for the back door.

This kid was good. She had all the instincts of a politician.

"Okay, here!" I said, throwing the third piece of gum on the floor by the other two. "But that's all!"

To make sure there would be no further negotiations, I quickly climbed back on the cabinet and returned the gum to its hiding place—but not before I took three pieces for myself. After all, I had masterminded this crime, why should I settle for just the one piece I had originally set out to get?

But as I watched my sister gathering her gum off the floor, I had my doubts about who the *real* mastermind was.

We were afraid to hide the gum in case it was discovered, so we each chewed all three pieces at once. Needless to say, we each had such a huge wad of gum that neither one of us could chew it.

By now, we were both so caught up in our venture to the darker side of life that throwing away the gum had become unthinkable.

We decided to mix the two wads together to see how far it would stretch.

Have you ever noticed in the movies when something bad is happening, the characters start moving in slow motion? Well, if you're ever in a situation where it takes more than ten seconds to blink—get outta there!

When I look back to that afternoon, I see my sister and me moving in slow motion—sticking the gum on our bedroom wall—*strrrrretching* it across the room, above the bed, into my brother's room, over his bed, and finally sticking it to the far wall in his room.

And I can see us standing there, our mouths dropping open in slow motion, our eyes slowly widening in horror as the gum, stretched to capacity, sagged leisurely down across the floor, draped over the bed, back down on the floor, into my brother's room, across his bed, and finally along his floor to the wall.

After the gum settled, everything stopped. When Malvina and I finally dared to look at each other, we both realized what we had to do. We began cleaning as though our lives depended on it—and they just about did! We were moving in fast motion like those old-time movies, faster and faster, like some out-of-control movie projector.

The big cleaning problem was the chenille bedspread on our bed. That chenille was so fluffy, you would almost disappear when you sat on it, and it embraced that gum like a long lost friend.

I finally had to get the scissors and cut a small—and I hoped unnoticeable—path across the bedspread.

Amazingly enough, my mother never did notice the missing gum or the coiffed bedspread. But our crime did not go unpunished.

For weeks after that, we kept waiting to get caught. It was like waiting for the other shoe to fall. We were edgy and suspicious of each other. What if one of us broke and confessed? The confessor would most certainly get off more lightly.

The bedspread was by far my biggest worry. Every time it was washed and hung on the line, I just *knew* my handiwork would come to light. Sometimes I wondered if it wouldn't be better to just confess, take my paddling, and get it over with.

I never did that, but every time I watched James digging tar out of the sidewalk, I envied his peace of mind.

As children of God, we're going to get into sticky situations from time to time. We don't plan it that way, but sometimes that forbidden box of gum reaches out and grabs us. The next thing we know, we're up to our ears in gum and chenille.

Instead of trimming the chenille, it would behoove us to remember what the apostle John said: "We have one who speaks to the Father in our defense—Jesus Christ, the Righteous One" (1 John 2:1).

Eee-i-ee-i-Ouch!

When my husband Len and I made our big move to the country, we went with visions of a quiet, genteel, country life. Our children would have incredibly rosy cheeks from breathing all that fresh air and eating all those home-grown veggies. There would be fresh bread from the oven, fresh milk from the cow, and fresh eggs from the chickens. What we didn't think about was that all that fresh stuff didn't just happen—it had to be weeded, baked, milked, and gathered.

By the time we got through milking, weeding, baking, and gathering, "genteel" was out the window.

Besides that, there was nothing "genteel" about the roads. We left pieces of our car up and down that road every time we went to town. But that wasn't such a bad thing, because we lived so far out of town that when we first moved out there I kept getting lost. It worked kind of like Hansel and Gretel. I'd go to town and then just follow my car parts home. Sometimes I'd follow the wrong car parts and end up at a strange house, but that was a great way to meet the neighbors.

Well, maybe I'm exaggerating just a little, but one thing I'm not exaggerating is our first winter out there. It was the worst winter that anyone could remember. It sleeted every day for several weeks. The temperature stayed around five or six degrees in the daytime and dipped below zero at night. It was awful!

By that time we had managed to become the proud owners of a calf, two pigs, six rabbits, three dogs, and we probably would have added a partridge in a pear tree to the menagerie if Len had thought about it. I say "Len" because he's the one who wanted all those farm animals. I wanted a dog and two goldfish—and maybe a partridge in a pear tree, but not cows and pigs and all those things old McDonald had, because I'll tell you something else old McDonald had—a tired wife.

At first, Len enjoyed those animals and took care of them—until he slipped on the ice and broke his arm. He had to have surgery on his elbow and was in the hospital for three days.

Now, I am a very sympathetic person, and I felt sorry for him when it happened because I know it really did hurt. But by the time his three-day hitch in the hospital was over, the truth of the situation had begun to sink in, and I really thought about breaking his other arm.

Our son, Jim, was in the second grade and Chris, our daughter, was eighteen months old. The second day that Len was in the hospital, Chris got sick and I had to take her to the doctor, pick Jim up from school, take them to my sister's house in town, and then go back out and feed old McDonald's menagerie, which took me until after dark to finish.

So by the time Len was able to come home, with a cast up to his shoulder and instructions to stay in the house until the sleet and ice melted, I knew that unless those animals learned to brown-bag it, I had a whole new world waiting for me. I also figured out that in that song about Old McDonald, his wife wrote the part that says "ee-i-ee-i-oh"!

The cold weather made taking care of the animals harder than usual because their drinking water would freeze. Since there was no water in the barnyard area, I had to haul water back and forth in a bucket twice a day. If I could have put the same number of miles on a motor home that I put walking back and forth to the barn, carrying water, I could have seen the entire United States and half of Canada—and kept my feet dry while I did it.

The calf was the biggest problem—literally. That calf was six months old and weighed around seven hundred pounds. I'm talking twenty-eight hundred quarter-pounders here. You know that ad where they sing about having your burger your way? Well, maybe at their drive-thru window, but when those burgers are on the hoof, it's a different story.

If I'd had it my way, that calf would have carried its own bucket to my back door and asked for a drink of water. As it was, it did go to the back door, but it didn't take the bucket, and it didn't go to my back door but to my neighbor's.

My neighbor called and told me the calf was in her backyard. Her husband was at work, and she was under the care of a chiropractor and wondered if I was going to be able to catch it myself.

By then, I had done so many things by myself for the first time, I didn't really think about it. I just got the rope and started out the door.

"You don't know how to rope a calf!" Len exclaimed, not believing what he was seeing.

"So, what's your point?" I asked a bit tersely, hoping he was about to tell me that he had trained that calf to go to the barn if we whistled.

He thought for a minute and then said, rather lamely, "Throw a wide loop."

That wasn't the answer I'd hoped for.

I stood there for a minute, thinking. Len thought I was thinking about how to throw a wide loop over the calf, but I wasn't. I was visualizing him stranded in the middle of the desert with nothing but day-old bread and peanut butter—no jelly.

There were ten acres of brush and gullies between our house and our neighbor's house. I trudged over there and, as I approached her backyard, I saw her standing by her back door, the calf a few yards away eyeballing the situation.

I made a wide loop in the rope and walked slowly toward the calf, wanting to get as close to it as I could. Much to my surprise, it just stood there, looking at me.

I walked right up to it and slipped the rope around its neck as though I did that sort of thing all the time.

The look on my neighbor's face was great! She was as surprised as I was, but I wasn't letting my surprise show. I was so casual about it, I impressed even myself.

I wanted to say something like, "So, what did you expect, Pilgrim?"

But instead I said, "Why are you having to see a chiropractor?"

I didn't get to hear her answer because about that time the calf was hit with a sudden wave of homesickness. It took off at a dead run for our barn, via ten acres of gullies and brush.

I had wrapped the rope around my wrist for a better hold when I had thought I would be "walking" the calf home. Big mistake.

Bouncing along behind that calf, I spent most of the trip on my posterior rather than on my feet.

I called out to the neighbor what I hoped was a nonchalant, "Bye!" but I think the nonchalance was lost in the translation.

And as for finding out why my neighbor had to see the chiropractor, I could find that out when I called her to get his name and phone number.

I learned several things that winter—and that particular day I think I learned why John Wayne walked the way he did.

Walking with the Lord soothes a lot of the bruises and scrapes we get from being dragged through life's gullies and brush.

"In all your ways acknowledge him, and he will make your paths straight" (Proverbs 3:6).

We're In The Dough, Now

When I was growing up, our kitchen pantry looked like a health food store. My dad would bring home armloads of vitamins and all kinds of jars of things that smelled terrible and tasted worse. We had seaweed, kelp, protein stuff, green stuff, and brown stuff, and ...

But he was sort of the Jekyll and Hyde of the cuisine world, because anytime you looked under his car seat, you could find candy wrappers, empty doughnut sacks, and so forth. I think his theory was that junk food was only unhealthy if you ate it in front of anyone. Or if you ate a salad, it would counteract the effects of a double chocolate fudge sundae.

I wish it worked that way because I could really make that theory work. For instance, ice cream is made from milk, which comes from a cow that eats grass that, to a cow, is salad. For that matter, chocolate and sugar both come from plants ... This line of thinking could open up a whole new world. With enough thought, this theory could soon put chocolate fudge sundaes right up there with carrot sticks in the food pyramid!

My dad never put it quite like this, but I think the message he wanted to convey to his family was, "Don't eat like I do, eat like I should."

Every now and then he'd get on what we would call one of his "health food kicks." He would decide that something we were doing wasn't healthy or that something we weren't doing was healthy, and he would make the necessary, albeit temporary, adjustments for us. And they always were temporary because they never lasted more than a couple of days before things would get back to "normal" again.

One of his worst decisions was the homemade bread deal. Now, I love homemade bread, and I even make it for my family, but too much of even a good thing is still . . . too much.

He decided that the preservatives in store-bought bread were unhealthy, and he was right. I don't disagree with that, but he wanted us to bake twelve loaves at a time and freeze them. Too much of a good thing!

The night he brought home the twelve bread pans and made the announcement, I knew I wasn't going to like the second part of the news, because when he said we'd need to make twelve loaves at a time, he looked at me.

I was around seventeen or eighteen at the time, and making twelve loaves of bread actually wouldn't have been that big of a deal, except I was also baby-sitting my youngest sister who was four, my four-year-old niece, my three-year-old niece, and my two-year-old nephew. And that made *everything* a big deal.

It was August and we didn't have air-conditioning, which contributed to the problem that was about to arise. And when I say "arise," no pun is intended. If ever a word described a problem, *arise* did.

On that fateful, bread-baking day, I fixed lunch for the kids and then put them all down for their naps before I even attempted to start baking a dozen loaves of bread.

I was in such a hurry to get as much of the bread done as possible before the kids woke up that, without thinking that each recipe made two loaves, I multiplied the recipe by twelve instead of six. So I had made enough dough for twenty-four loaves instead of twelve.

If that dough had been "dough," I'd have been a multi-millionaire.

The heat in the kitchen made that dough rise so fast it was like a living, breathing thing—with a social life—very busy, with things to do and places to go. It was "on the rise," and no mere mortal could stop it. Today, Dallas; tomorrow, the world!

I imagined my family's coming home from work and finding no sign of me except for the soles of my feet protruding from a giant glob of dough that had completely taken over the kitchen. And after digging me out, they would discover a rolling pin in my hand and a smile on my face because I had fought a good fight and, thanks to my dad, had left this world totally healthy!

Naturally there would be book and movie rights to consider, and before it was over, *Attack of the Killer Bread Dough* would become a classic right up there with *Moby Dick* and *Casablanca*.

But when my family came home, they didn't find the kitchen encased in dough, and they certainly didn't find me with a smile on my face.

There was dough in every pan and bowl in the house and it was still growing. By the time the bread in the oven was ready to take out, the dough waiting to go in had already swelled out and over the top of the pans.

The kids had all gotten up from their naps and were only too happy to "help." The sight that met their eyes when they came into the kitchen was better than any sandbox or mud-pie operation they had ever seen.

Thinking I could keep them out of the main mess, I gave each of them a piece of dough to play with at one end of the table. That worked about as well as trying to keep ants out of a picnic by setting a separate plate for them.

There were flour and dough in the house where flour and dough had never been before. There were little flour footprints in the living room and little flour handprints on the couch and on the telephone and on every doorknob in the house. Even the dog, who had been watching the action through the back screen door, had flour streaked under one eye. I never did figure out how that happened. Except for the volcanic temperature, our house had taken on sort of a winter wonderland look.

The only things in that house that looked more astonishing than the kitchen were the looks on the faces of everyone who walked in that day. They all stood there, speechless, with their eyebrows raised and their mouths hanging open. I took one look at everyone just standing there looking at me, and I burst into tears.

It didn't take Mother too long to figure out what had happened.

When it was all over, we had enough bread and cinnamon rolls and dinner rolls to open a bakery.

When we finished the rolls and bread, we still had a big hunk of dough left, so my sister-in-law concocted a brand-new recipe; one never before—and never since—attempted.

A few days before, we had bought a bushel of pears, and Mother had cooked a huge pan of them with sugar, cinnamon, and butter to eat however anyone wanted to eat them.

My sister-in-law rolled that hunk of dough out, and we filled it full of the cooked pears. Then she pulled it all together and sealed it like a giant turnover. She put her hands under one end of it, I got the other end, and we lifted it carefully into the turkey roaster. It was so full of pears that when we dropped it into the pan it made a "plopping" sound. So we called it "Pear Plop." It was really very good. But we never made it again because it takes a certain amount of dough to hold enough pears to make the "plopping" sound essential for "Pear Plop," and I never want to see that much dough again!

Before the last loaf of bread had even come out of the oven, my dad had decided that homemade bread was only healthy occasionally, and then only in small amounts.

When the Lord told Satan that "Man does not live by bread alone," I know He meant things other than bread, but I can look back to that day and it sort of puts an exclamation mark on that verse for me.

This Little Piggy
Went to Day Care

One year my sister Malvina and I merged our energies and opened a day-care business at her house. It was very successful—we had several kids, and we really worked to make it go.

We had craft classes for them, hot lunches, and kindergarten pick-up and delivery. All in all, it was a working mom's dream, if I say so myself. It was also our dream, because having a successful, home-based business was something we had both always wanted.

But the dream soon took on nightmare characteristics, and not just your run-of-the-mill type nightmares. I'm talking Freddy Krueger, here.

It started with our decision to sell homemade candy. Now, I'll be the first to admit that the candy business probably wouldn't have caused a problem by itself; the pig was the big problem—even though it was a small pig. But I'm getting ahead of myself.

It was Christmas time, and we had this great family recipe for a date nut candy log that we decided to try to sell for extra Christmas money.

In the afternoons, when the kids were having their naps, my sister would take candy samples to give out in the stores and get orders for the candy. I would stay with the kids and make candy to fill the orders we already had. It was working out great.

Then one afternoon Malvina was out getting orders, the kids were napping, and I was up to my ears in date nut candy when the phone rang. When I answered it, my husband's voice said, in an overly cheerful tone, "Hi! What are you doing?"

I couldn't understand why he was asking me that; he knew what I was doing.

"Well," I said, flicking a crumb of candy off my shoulder, "for the last hour I've been soaking in a warm bubble bath, and now I'm sitting here waiting for the maid to finish fixing my lunch."

He laughed and made small talk for a few minutes until finally, he said, "Well, I've got to get back to work. Oh, by the way, I got a pig today."

"By the way, you got a pig today?" I repeated.

"Yeah, I was going to surprise you, but I couldn't wait. So, what do you think?"

"Flowers would have been nice," I said.

"Honey, this was such a good deal, I couldn't pass it up," he said.

"But it's Christmas time, how can we afford a pig?"

"That's the best part! It was free!"

"Free?" I said, almost afraid to ask the rest of the question. "Why would anyone give away a pig? And even if it was free, we don't have a pig house or a fence or anything."

"It's not called a pig house, it's called a pigsty," he said, his voice dripping with patience.

"Why was it free and where are we keeping it?" I said, my voice totally devoid of patience.

"Let me explain before you get upset. This is a very small pig ..."

"So, where are we going to keep a very small pig?" I asked.

There was a long enough pause to cause my apprehension level to hit TILT.

"We'll have to keep it in the house for a while," he finally managed to say.

Now, keep in mind, this happened several years before people started keeping miniature pigs as pets. This happened when a pig was a pig and by any other name was still a pig.

"No!"

"Honey, it's so tiny! It's in a shoe box!"

"No, no, no, NO!"

"Its mother rejected it," he said.

"I don't blame her," I answered.

"We'll talk about it this evening. I've got to get back to work. Bye," he said, and I was left listening to the dial tone.

The first thing Len did when we got home that night was to take the pig out of the box and give it to me to hold. This man was a real pro. He knew exactly what he was doing. That pig really *was* so tiny that it was in a shoe box, and it *was* really cute. There I was, holding that sweet, little pig while I told Len how impossible it would be to take care of one so small.

He reached over and took the pig from me, saying, "You're right. I don't know what I was thinking. This pig would require way too much care, and neither one of us has that much time."

"What are you going to do with it?" I asked, hoping he would say he knew of a home for pigs.

"It'll have to be destroyed," he said, putting on his jacket.

"No!" I yelled, snatching the pig from him with all the ferocity of an enraged mama pig who was protecting her own.

"But, honey, there's no way you'll have time to do this."

"Yes, I will, I will."

"Okay, if you're sure," he said, taking an eyedropper out of his coat pocket. "You can feed it with this. I'll set the

31

alarm to go off every two hours so it won't miss a feeding. Goodnight, little mama."

As I watched him disappear down the hall and into our bedroom, my motherly instincts suddenly began to wane. He will never know how close he came to getting hit in the back of the head with a flying pig.

The next morning I got up with circles under my eyes from three nighttime feedings. I felt guilty because the last time I fed the pig, I found myself mentally measuring it for a hoagie bun.

After I had a couple of cups of coffee to get my nerve geared up, I called my sister to try and explain why I was going to have to bring a pig with me that morning.

"I think this is going to be one of those days," she said, laughing. "I thought you just said you were bringing a pig with you."

"I did say that," I said.

"What do you mean, 'a pig'?" she asked, still not realizing I meant a PIG.

"It's a baby pig, and I have to bring it with me because it has to be fed every two hours."

"No!"

"It's a very small pig," I said.

"No! No! No!"

"Its mother rejected it."

Talk about role reversal! I was playing Len, my sister was playing me, and the pig was playing an innocent bystander.

"Look," she said, "even if it is a small pig we can't keep it here because if the parents find out we're keeping a pig in the house, they'll take their kids out of day care. And when word gets around, our candy sales are history."

I hadn't thought of that.

"I just don't know what to do about it," I said.

She thought for a minute and then she said, "Okay, bring it with you, and when you get here, honk the horn. I'll get the kids busy in the other end of the house while you sneak the pig down into the basement."

That plan came off without a hitch. It worked perfectly! It was such a success that after the pig was safely hidden in the basement, I had a tremendous feeling of exhilaration, as if we had just pulled off the hoax of the century. You'd have thought we were dealing with the CIA instead of a group of five-year-olds.

Well, we set the timer on the oven to go off every two hours, and when it buzzed, Malvina would get the kids' attention so I could run down to the basement and feed the pig. This was pretty exhausting, but it worked.

But by that afternoon, my sister was beginning to run out of things with which to distract the kids, and they were beginning to look at her as if maybe she was ready for the Big Day Care Center in the sky.

In between feedings we were catching up on our candy orders. The recipe was incredibly hard to mix since it had chopped dates, marshmallows, pecans, and graham cracker crumbs—it was like trying to mix cold tar.

That afternoon we managed to mix, roll, and wrap thirty-two of those candy logs. We felt as if we had been pulled through a knothole backward, but we also had a tremendous feeling of accomplishment.

Until . . .

While we were standing there admiring our thirty-two date nut rolls stacked like cordwood on the cabinet, I discovered a button missing from my cuff—a button that hadn't been missing when I started mixing the candy.

We searched every nook and cranny in the house, from kitchen to basement. That was the most intense game of "button, button, who's got the button?" that either one of us had ever played.

But it was to no avail. Finally, we both stood mutely staring at the only place we hadn't searched, the thirty-two candy rolls, stacked like cordwood on the cabinet.

"Do you think it's in one of those?" my sister asked in a very tired, lackluster voice.

"Maybe," I said with about one degree less enthusiasm than she was registering.

There was a long silence.

"So, what now?" I asked.

She just stood there shaking her head for the longest time. I was beginning to think she had developed some sort of nervous tic. Maybe the weight of that missing button was the proverbial "straw that broke the camel's back."

Then she began laughing, quietly at first, like it was some private joke only she knew about. Then the laughter got louder and louder, and the tears began to run down her face and she was gasping for breath.

"What?" I asked, laughing just because she was.

But she couldn't answer. She wasn't even making a sound now. Her mouth was open, and she was obviously laughing, but with a temporary loss of sound.

The harder she laughed, the harder I laughed, until we were both sitting on the floor, almost helpless with laughter.

Finally she said, as she tried desperately to catch her breath, "I know what to do about the candy."

I was laughing too hard to even ask what she had in mind.

But that was all right, she didn't need a straight line, she was on a roll.

"When we deliver the candy, we'll tell them that we hid a button in one of the candy rolls and the person who gets the candy with the button wins a pig!"

That was too much. Everything became a blur of pigs, buttons, candy, and kids, and we laughed and laughed and laughed. After that, we felt sooooo much better!

We decided to go ahead and take a chance on delivering the candy, and that was good because a couple of days later we found the button in the silverware drawer.

Unfortunately, the little pig was too young and it didn't make it, but if it had survived, I don't know what we would have done with it. It would definitely have been a pet. We'd have ended up sharing our television and snacks every evening with a three-hundred-pound couch potato.

God is such a good God, and He has put us together in a wonderful and awesome way. When our nose tickles, He has given us the ability to sneeze. When we're tired, He has given us the pleasure of a good, deep yawn. And when things go wrong, He has given us the ability to sit back and laugh at ourselves—and that is definitely wonderful and awesome!

"May the God of hope fill you with all joy and peace as you trust in him" (Romans 15:13).

Those Little-Town Blues

When I was younger, I had plans to set the world on fire, but as I dealt with life on a day-in, day-out basis, I discovered that just a wiener roast in my own backyard wasn't such a bad idea.

By the time I met my husband, I was still gathering kindling for when I would get this blazing fire started. I had lived in a very large city for eighteen years when I met him. We were married, and after a couple of years, we bought our first home there. I loved living in the city, and I thought we'd be there forever.

There's just something about living in a big city that makes you feel like a part of the mainstream of life. I think part of it may be that you get such a satisfaction and a feeling of accomplishment every time you make it home from work without getting creamed on the freeway.

Well, a year after we bought our house, Len got laid off from work. Our son was two years old, and we had to make some unexpected changes in our plans for where and how we would raise our family.

Now, if the Lord had asked for my opinion about where He'd planned for us to live, I'd have said to Him, "You've gotta be kidding!"

He didn't ask. And He wasn't kidding. Instead, He opened up an opportunity for us to move to a small town two hundred miles away from our families, where Len started an appliance repair business.

It all happened so fast, and it was such a drastic change, we almost got the bends. We moved from a place with four lanes of bumper-to-bumper traffic, to a place where people stopped their cars in the middle of the street to visit with other people, who stopped *their* cars in the middle of the street.

The first time I witnessed this phenomenon of street visiting, I couldn't figure out why they had stopped. When I discovered it was to visit with each other, I couldn't figure what in the world they had to talk about. I think the Lord smiled, shook His head and said, "You still don't get it, do you? But you will."

And, eventually, I did get it, but not for a while. I thought I would curl up and die, I was so miserable. I missed the noise of the city—katydids, tree frogs, and owls were no substitute for car horns, loud engines, and screeching brakes. The quiet stillness of the night was louder than anything I had ever heard in the city.

The first time I took a breath of fresh air, my lungs panicked. Then came the carbon monoxide withdrawals.

I had visions of what it would be like to spend New Year's Eve in this place. First we would go to town and walk up and down in front of the bakery, smelling the fresh bread. Then we would hurry over to the drugstore where we would get a seat on the wooden bench out front and watch the bank clock across the street as it blinked the time and temperature. Then, when it blinked midnight, we'd all stand up and sing "Auld Lang Syne" while the band from the Golden Leaf Rest Home played "My Wild Irish Rose."

And I think the Lord shook His head and said, "You still don't get it, do you? But you will."

Sure enough, I did get it, but it happened so gradually that I didn't even notice. One afternoon, I was sitting in the porch swing; my son had just finished lunch and was deep into his afternoon nap. It was so quiet, the only noise was the swing creaking on its chains. Then the whistle at the flour mill blew, as it did every day at noon—kind of a deep, bellowing sound that can be heard all over town. Soon after, the church bells began chiming hymns as they did every day at noon. When they finished, it was all quiet, save for the creaking of the swing. I felt so peaceful and content. I guess that was the first time I told the Lord how much I appreciated His bringing us to this place.

And I think the Lord said, "Didn't I tell you so?"

Thou Shalt Not Imply

When our kids were small, my husband and I got into a business that would supposedly not only give us extra income but could quite possibly make us multimillionaires. But in order to hit the multimillionaire level, we needed to bring other people into the business.

There was one couple who didn't want to join until they saw physical evidence that Len and I were on our way to being guests on *Lifestyles of the Rich and Famous.*

So we left the "doubting Thomases" eating our dust as we raced down the yellow brick road leading to our pot of gold. But before we could finish the race, our car broke down. Actually, it didn't "break down": It totally expired. And that was a problem, because at that point, we were still a couple million dollars short of having a couple million dollars.

We needed a car that was attractive, reliable, and affordable. It was like looking for prime rib on a bologna budget.

Finally, after looking under a thousand hoods and kicking four thousand tires, we found a great deal on a little sports car convertible with a brand-new black top. Now we didn't want a sports car convertible, but the price was right, so ...

When I say "little sports car," I mean teeny-tiny little sports car. My husband is 6'3", and the top of that car came to about his waist. The first time we drove it to church and people saw Len, both of our kids, and me climbing out of that car, they looked at us as if we were a bunch of clowns at the circus who had just emerged from a miniature Model T. When church was over, they gathered around again to see how we all got in there.

We bought the car in February, and Len told me that it was going to have to be my Valentine's Day gift, because now he couldn't afford a box of chocolates. That was fine with me. I really loved the little car.

Well, one Saturday evening in May, I drove the car to the grocery store, and there stood the doubting Thomases. The first thing they wanted to know was how our business was doing.

Now I could have said that we were still plugging along, but I didn't. Instead, I heard myself saying, as I pointed to the car, "Well, I'll show you how we're doing—see what my husband got me for Valentine's Day."

I told myself at the time that it wasn't a lie, it was an implication. Well, that night, and I mean that very night, God showed me what He thought of my implication.

We lived in a trailer house, and we didn't have a garage or a carport. That night, we had the worst hailstorm I have ever seen in my whole life! When it was over, my car looked like it had been attacked by giant razor blades! The beautiful, new convertible top was ripped all to pieces.

God is a loving parent and He disciplines with love as well as compassion. The body of the car didn't have a single dent in it, but our insurance didn't cover hail damage. We couldn't afford to put another top on it until September, so we had to drive the car with the top down for four months.

Upon arrival at my every destination, my hair looked like I had stuck my finger in a light socket. We tried not to get caught in the rain, but once we were caught out on the highway in a real gully washer! Let me tell you, we made a lot of hearts "merry" that day. People were passing us and laughing their heads off.

By the time September rolled around and we were able to replace the top, we didn't have to imply anything to anybody; most people had figured it out for themselves.

I do want to add a "PS" to this: The day after the hailstorm, I went to check the damage done to the green onions in my garden and there wasn't so much as a broken stem. God is a loving Father. And those onions were the best I've ever eaten!

We Really Got Her Goat

My husband, Len, and I enjoy trying new foods—we've tried everything from alligator to zucchini. So when a friend of ours told us that he had eaten some barbecued goat meat and how delicious it was, my husband wouldn't rest until he tried it.

I couldn't quite warm up to the idea of eating a goat; the thought of it just didn't make my mouth water.

"Goat meat was eaten in biblical times," Len told me.

"So? John the Baptist ate locust, but I'll pass on that one, too," I replied.

After several of these exchanges, I reluctantly agreed that if he could find a goat, I'd try a bite. I didn't really think it would be that easy to locate a goat . . . I mean, how many Southern-fried goat places could there be?

But a few days later, he came home with wonderful news. He had bought a goat from a lady in the country. The goat was being processed that very minute, and in a couple of days it would be little white packages in our freezer.

I shuddered at the thought of it, but when he came home with the packages, they looked just like meat from the grocery store.

That night we barbecued some of it and, lo and behold, it was excellent! I don't think it was eaten with barbecue sauce in biblical times, but it was sure good anyway.

A couple of months passed. The goat was gone and forgotten—except whenever we barbecued, I would think about the goat, and my mouth would water.

Our son, Jim, was in the fourth grade, and we were up to our ears in Little League baseball. I would take him to practice and, since we lived several miles away, I'd wait for him at the ball field.

On one particular day, I was sitting in the bleachers when one of the other moms sat down by me and we struck up a conversation. After a few minutes of visiting, we introduced ourselves. When she found out my name she said, "Didn't your husband buy a goat from me a few months ago?

"Do you live on Kingsly Road?" I asked.

"Yes, I do."

We both laughed and commented on its being a small world. Then she dropped the bomb.

"How is Gerald?" she asked.

"Gerald?" I queried.

"The goat—Gerald," she replied.

Now you would think that the fact that the goat had a name would have given me a clue. But no, I just kept talking. "Oh! He's already all gone, but he was delicious. I was surprised to find out that goat meat is so good!"

"You—*ate*—him?" she asked, her eyes getting bigger and bigger as they filled with tears.

She told me that the goat had been the kids' pet, but they had gotten tired of taking care of him. She thought Len had bought him as a pet for *our* kids.

When I realized what had happened, I felt like a cannibal.

I apologized over and over. All in all, she was very gracious about it, but she never sat by me again. I got the feeling she didn't want to socialize with a savage.

When I got home, I told Len what had happened, and he told me he thought she knew what we were going to do with the goat.

I don't know, maybe barbecued locusts would have been better.

By the way, it's good to know that there won't be any goats in heaven, only His sheep!

"All the nations will be gathered before him, and he will separate the people one from another as a shepherd separates the sheep from the goats" (Matthew 25:32).

Redundancy Alert

I was noticing on my word processor that one of its features is called the "Words Redundancy Check." Now think about that. We have finally become intelligent enough to build a machine that tells us when we're talking too much.

It's too bad we can't build something like that into our heads so that when we've said enough, a silent alarm goes off and our mouths automatically slam shut. However, speaking for myself, it's probably best that I don't have the advantage of that. There are days when I'd have trouble finding a time when my mouth was open long enough to eat a meal.

And if there was a whole group of us "redundant talkers" together, the sound of mouths slamming shut would be deafening. We wouldn't dare go together to visit someone in the hospital.

My husband says that when I stop at a red light, the car full of total strangers in the next lane knows my family history by the time the light turns green. Now that statement is not only exaggerated, it comes from someone who also talks to traffic, but he uses words like "nincompoop," "road hog," and worst of all, "woman driver"!

I've noticed something about "redundant" words: they flow from our mouths with all the ease in the world, but when it comes time to eat them, they're really hard to swallow. At least they aren't fattening, and that's good, because I've sure eaten my share of foolish words.

I remember one time in particular. I was young and single and very impatient with anyone who wasn't young and single. I was working in a large plant in Dallas, and I rode to work every day in a carpool of older married ladies. When I say "older," I mean they were probably in their early forties, but at that time forty, to me, was nothing short of ancient. I thought of them in terms of old and boring, and they thought of me in terms of young and ridiculous ... which, looking back now, I guess was absolutely accurate.

Anyhow, I was finally able to buy a car. It was an old one, but it was mine. I told the lady whose car I had been riding in that I would be leaving the carpool the next week since I had bought myself a car.

She asked me if I'd be interested in carpooling with my car; I'd drive one week and she'd drive one week. Now, you have to understand, I pictured myself as a real swinging-single woman on the move, with places to go and things to do. In reality, that was true, but those places to go and things to do wouldn't have interfered with carpooling, because K-mart and Washateria both stayed open late.

But I told her in a very condescending tone of voice that I didn't really want to be tied down with riders because I never knew when I'd want to go someplace after work. REDUNDANCY ALERT!

The next week, my first day to drive alone, I pulled up to a stop sign on a long, open stretch of road and, looking in my rearview mirror, I saw that they were behind me, and they were laughing at my car. My car was a used one, but it didn't look used. Actually, it look misused. But still . . .

So I thought to myself, *Okay, ladies, eat my dust!* I peeled out like I was driving the Indy 500. When I did, my muffler fell off. I had never seen a muffler before, so I didn't know what that thing was that was dragging on the pavement and making all that noise. I just knew that something wasn't working right.

Then the ladies pulled up beside me, but they weren't laughing as they had been. Now they were hysterical. They had tears running down their faces and they couldn't catch their breath. I've never seen anyone enjoy a muffler so much.

When they finally collected their composure, they asked if I needed a ride to work and back home again ... unless, of course, I had other plans. At that time, my only plans were to try and learn to keep my mouth shut and my exhaust system intact.

Solomon said it all very well in Proverbs 25:11—"A word aptly spoken is like apples of gold in setting of silver."

I've got to remember that.

Do You Think
Anyone Noticed?

When I was a freshman in college, we had to go through several months of initiation by the upperclassmen. While it was all great fun, it wasn't something we could take lightly and just do if we were in the mood. If they told us to do anything, anything at all, we had to do it or pay the consequences—which were always much worse than the original "request."

I didn't mind most of the things. Some of them were a little embarrassing sometimes, but for the most part, I really didn't mind.

But there was one thing we had to do that I dearly hated. At every football game, we had to run out on the field at halftime and form a victory line for the boys to pass through as they returned for the second half of the game.

And when I say "run," I mean *run*. We weren't allowed to walk across that field at all.

Now, this was so many years ago that I can't remember if we were required to dress up or if it was just something we chose to do. Things were quite different than they are now. Today, college kids would never even dream of wearing three-inch heels to a football game. I think college kids today are a little more laid back and relaxed than we were.

At any rate, we were all dressed up for the game that night, high-heeled shoes and all. It had rained all day, and the football field was a loblolly of mud.

I have seen women who can walk in three-inch heels with queenly elegance. They could run across a muddy football field with the grace of a fleeing gazelle. Unfortunately, I am not one of those people.

I looked more like an ostrich loping across the field that night. I kept saying to myself, over and over, *I will not fall down, I will not fall down, I WILL NOT fall down!*

Of course, I did fall down, but, believe it or not, it had nothing in the world to do with my high heels. And it wasn't your everyday, run-of-the-mill fall—the Roman Empire didn't fall as hard as I did on that football field in front of a stadium full of people.

I made it across the field to form the victory line with the other freshmen. Then I managed to make it back across the field again and was almost safely out of sight when I discovered the hard way that they had moved the chain they use to mark off yardage.

I never did understand why no one else made that "trip." We were all running in a group. Everyone else had to cross over that hidden chain before I did, because I was last, since running has never been my cup of tea. But everyone else seemed to know it was there. I got the feeling that the people who marked the yardage said to each other, "Okay, let's tell everyone to watch out for the chain except that girl who runs like an ostrich."

The chain caught me across the front of my ankles and it was like a giant, invisible hand yanking my feet out from under me. I slid on my stomach in the mud, plowing up the ground with my face as I went. I came to a stop when my head met the corrugated metal fence at the edge of the field. The entire length that I slid was no more than three or four feet, but it seemed like a mile. And I don't think I could have made a deeper furrow in the mud if I had been on a John Deere tractor.

I'll never forget the way that fence sounded when I hit it. It was kind of an echoing, vibrating *Boinnnnng-ing-ing*. The policeman standing there tried to help me up, but it was so slick we both kept slipping back down.

I was really grateful he was there to help me up, but from the look on his face and the mud on his uniform, I think I was a lot happier about it than he was.

When I went to the game that night, I had no idea I was going to be the halftime entertainment. One thing's for sure, show business is *not* what it's cracked up to be.

When I got back to my seat, I had to ask the upper-classmen for permission to leave the game and go back to the dorm to shower and change clothes. They joyfully denied permission. I had to sit for the remainder of the game, covered from head to toe with mud.

Ever since Adam and Eve got themselves ousted from the garden, humans have been known to plow up the ground with their noses from time to time. It seems like just when we think we've got it made, somebody moves the chain!

But the good news is that every time we take a nosedive, God is standing by to pick us up, and He always washes the mud off right then. He never makes us carry it around all day. "Though your sins are like scarlet, they shall be as white as snow" (Isaiah 1:18).

Hooray for the Fifth of July!

Ilove the fifth of July! In fact, I look forward to it so much, I wish they would make it another holiday. On the fifth of July, I celebrate the Fourth of July's being over.

Don't misunderstand me. I'm very patriotic—I even cry at parades. But on the fifth of July, all of the hoopla is over, the watermelon seeds have been washed off the porch, the fireworks are silenced, and the final finger and toe count has confirmed that everyone is still in one piece.

The Fourth of July is good, but the fifth of July is better.

That's just the way *I* feel about the Fourth. My husband has a totally different view of it. To me, it's the Fourth of July. To him, it's THE FOURTH OF JULY!!!

Seventeen years ago, he built a black powder cannon, and every Fourth of July he drags it out and fires it. Not once, not twice, not TEN times, but ... *all ... day ... loooooong*!

Our dogs hate being boarded at the vet when we go out of town, but when they see Len setting the cannon up, they climb over each other trying to get into the car, begging me to take them to the vet for a sleep over. Last year, one of them even offered to drive.

The cannon has the same effect on our neighbors. I've watched neighbors move in and out over the years, and I've noticed that most of the moving takes place either right before or right after the Fourth of July.

The first year Len had the cannon, the neighbors who lived at the end of our road came to our house to see what in the world was going on. They went back home with their ears ringing and a firm resolve to be out of town on the next Fourth of July.

That first year was a learning experience for our neighbors and for Len. He was using a great deal of caution with that black powder, but too much of a good thing—even caution—can backfire. And believe me, when black powder is involved, you don't want anything to backfire, not even caution.

Being overly cautious almost caused Len to blow himself into the next county. I think the angels God had watching Len that night are still shaking their heads in disbelief.

He had bought a huge can of black powder to use for that first, memorable Fourth of July, when the world would be introduced to The Cannon. But it only took one capful of powder to fire the cannon, so at the end of the day he still had half of that can of powder left.

Our kids were both young, and he didn't feel comfortable having a can of black powder setting anyplace on the property, for fear of an accident. He decided the rest of the powder should be destroyed. I think it was probably at this point that the angels knew they had their work cut out for them.

It was around midnight, and we were all tired—even the kids were ready for the fifth of July to come. Except for the moon and stars, it was pretty dark outside. Len poured the powder in a long line down the driveway and then . . .

He lit it.

Now, I've seen this done in the movies. On the big screen, when they light a trail of gunpowder, the fire calmly follows the powder until it reaches the end. In real life, it doesn't work like that.

When he bent over and stuck that match to the powder, it all went up at once! I've never seen anything quite like that . . . and I'll be perfectly content if I never see anything quite like it again.

First, it was dark and I could barely see him. Then he lit the match and suddenly there was a huge, blinding, white flash. The flash only lasted a split second, but in that split second—in that white flash—there was Len, posed to run. Then it was dark again.

It all happened so fast, I was still sitting there with my mouth open when Len walked over to me. His sideburns and eyebrows were gone, and he smelled like a singed chicken.

I was really relieved to see that, except for his sideburns and eyebrows, he was still intact. I felt a great relief to know that *now* we had surely seen the last of that cannon. Wrong!!

By the time the next Fourth of July rolled around, Len had grown new sideburns and eyebrows and was ready to launch his cannon again. Dogs and neighbors, beware!

As for me, I'm thankful we have something to celebrate on the Fourth of July, but we celebrate the best freedom of all at Christmas and Easter—and we don't need a cannon to do it! "Now the Lord is the Spirit, and where the Spirit of the Lord is, there is freedom" (2 Corinthians 3:17).

Boo!

Have you ever stopped to think about what women go through to look attractive . . . or what we deem as attractive? We cream, steam, fluff, and stuff.

We bleach our hair to find out if blondes really do have more fun, and we color it if we find out they don't. If it's curly, we straighten it. If it's straight, we curl it. If that old adage about the "grass being greener" is true, then it's twice as true when it comes to how we look.

We're never satisfied with ourselves. We nearly always think we have too much or not enough in one area or another. If we're not adding to, we're taking away.

And here's the funny part: After we get through rearranging and pummeling our bodies into whatever shape, size, or color we want, then we feel beautiful even if it doesn't quite work out that way. Beauty is in the eye of the beholder? It just depends on who is beholding what!

I remember one time when I was a single, working girl, I had spent the summer getting what I thought was the most gorgeous tan this side of the equator. I had fantasies about being contacted by a large cosmetic company to represent their suntan lotion. I visualized myself on billboards and TV and magazines, gazing out at an admiring public who would spare no expense to get a tan like mine.

But until word of my tan reached the cosmetic moguls, life went on, and I would have to content myself with letting the world admire my tan in person.

On this particular day, I decided I needed to stay in and clean out some cluttered dresser drawers while I gave myself a moisturizing facial.

I totally covered my face with a thick layer of facial cream and, wanting to keep it on for an hour, I began cleaning out my dresser drawers. It didn't matter that I looked like a panda bear peering out from behind that white mask—nobody was going to see me, anyhow.

Well, I got so involved in checking out old letters and photos and all of the memorabilia that I can get stuffed into a drawer, that I completely forgot about the cream on my face. That wouldn't have hurt anything, except I decided to go to the store and get new shelf paper to put in the bottom of the drawer.

I lived a couple of blocks from the shopping center, so I just hopped in my car for a quick trip down there. Normally, I'd have seen at least one person I knew who could have asked me what in the world I was doing out in public like that, but my friends must have had other plans that day. But I saw several people I didn't know, and they saw me. In fact, they didn't just see me. They looked. They stared. They gawked!

And the more they looked, stared, and gawked, the higher I held my head. I'm sure I added a little extra swing to my walk. And I thought to myself, *This has got to be the best tan I've ever had!*

When I went through the check-out stand, the young man at the cash register looked at me and smiled, but his smile got away from him until it was so broad I thought it was going to cover his ears.

I smiled back, picked up my sack of shelf paper and glided past the check-out stand in what I felt to be a very impressive, swan-like exit.

As I got to the door, I heard him explode in laughter. That was the first inkling I had that something wasn't right, but I still didn't figure it out.

When I got back home, I went right to the dresser to put the paper in the drawers. As I was opening the package, I glanced in the mirror over the dresser. . . .

I just stood there staring at the reflection of that person who was staring back at me from behind a thick, white, goop mask.

I said to myself, *I did not go to the store like that. I didn't, I didn't!* But I knew that I had.

It would be a long time before I showed my face around that store again. Not that it would matter—they wouldn't recognize me, anyway.

Needless to say, the cosmetic companies never contacted me, and as summer faded, so did my tan. But the memory of that trip to the shopping center never did fade. And while no one remembers my tan that year, they probably still remember my face in the store that day.

We wear so many masks for so many different occasions, that sometimes we don't even recognize ourselves. And most of the time people we meet don't see the "real" us— but our families do, bless their hearts.

They get to see us in the morning before our coffee. They get to see us in the evening after we've been notified our bank account is overdrawn, the transmission went out on the car, and our least favorite relatives in the world are coming to spend the entire month of August with us. They would probably appreciate some kind of a mask at that point!

Lord, help me to live in such a way that when people look at me, instead of seeing a mask, they'll get a glimpse of You.

Just Hop on My Back

The year my husband broke his arm, I had to take a crash course in animal husbandry. Up until that time, I had always thought animal husbandry meant learning how to deal with a cantankerous husband. But by the time Len was back full-steam, I knew what it really meant.

I did, however, discover that there really isn't that much difference between taking care of farm animals and taking care of a husband and kids. You feed and water them; you keep their living quarters shoveled out—and that's about the same thing you do for your farm animals.

There was one thing more I learned during this time: the fine art of mountain climbing. Now, my mountain was only eight feet high, but it might as well have been eight hundred feet high. And I didn't climb it "because it was there": I climbed it because *I* was there.

It was the day I brought Len home from the hospital. Those dirt roads were packed with ice and incredibly slick. I wasn't used to driving on them because before Len broke his arm, he always did the driving when it was icy. I did a lot of "backseat" driving, but believe me, the view is a lot different from the driver's seat than it is from the backseat.

Len discovered that, too. I'll bet the fingerprints of his one good hand are still imprinted in the dashboard of that truck.

I managed to slide the truck off into a ditch before we got home. Len was a little wild-eyed, but nobody was hurt; in fact, the kids wanted to do it again. The problem was, we were so far out in the boonies that we had to wait awhile before someone happened by to pull us out.

By the time we got home, it was nearly dark and I still had to feed and water the animals, which was about a two-hour job; the hard-packed ice made it almost impossible to stay on my feet, and, in view of Len's unfortunate "ice follies" performance, I needed to be extra careful. One broken bone was about all our household could handle.

It was bitter cold and pitch dark when I finished feeding the animals. As I inched my way down the hill to our trailer house, I was so grateful that it was my last trip for the night. I was numb with cold and kept imagining myself sitting in my kitchen, drinking a steaming cup of chicken noodle soup. Actually, I thought how nice it would be to have a big dishpan of hot chicken noodle soup to soak my feet in.

As I started to open the gate to our yard, I heard a pitiful whine. I turned around and saw our dog Sidney standing on the edge of our cellar hole, looking down at something that was really upsetting him.

Our cellar hole was just that: an eight-by-ten hole that was dug when they put in our water well. We planned to have it made into a cellar in the spring. The place that would eventually be the steps into the cellar was, at this point, just a steep incline of solid ice.

In the bottom of the hole was Sidney's true love, Minnie Mae. Minnie Mae was a big, beautiful German shepherd who belonged to the people down the road. She was crippled in her hind legs, which didn't hamper her running and jumping ability, but at that moment her condition definitely hampered her ability to climb out of that hole. She couldn't get the traction she needed.

Putting my noodle soup fantasy on hold, I got a rope and tied it to the fence post by the cellar hole, and, while Len stood in the doorway of the trailer, supervising the rescue mission, I lowered myself down the incline and into the hole. It was great! I felt just like some heroine on one of those Saturday afternoon TV shows. I mean, I had just lowered myself by rope into a dark hole to make a daring rescue! Move over, Wonder Woman!

But after I got down there, I realized that getting into the hole was as far as my plan went. Minnie Mae was happy to see me, but she gave me a look that said, "Okay, now what?"

Lifting her up and out was out of the question ... we were standing in an eight-foot hole. Besides, Minnie looked like a sausage with legs. She obviously enjoyed her doggy victuals.

I tried to get behind her and push her up the incline, but I couldn't get enough traction for that. My TV heroine character was beginning to take on cartoon characteristics.

The harder I tried, the more exhausted I became. Finally, I decided I'd go ahead and climb out, warm up a bit, and then call Minnie's family to come and help. I didn't know them, but after all, it was *their* dog.

Much to my surprise, I discovered that I was too pooped to pull myself back up the incline. That would have been all right if I had been a real TV heroine. Then the local TV hero would have been in the wings, waiting to leap into the dark, cold abyss to save me.

As it was, my hero was standing in the wings with his "wing in a sling," shouting instructions to me. Really good ones, too, like, "Pull harder!"

Maybe those instructions did help because with a final surge of determination, I held onto the rope and pulled myself ... halfway up. Then my feet slid out from under me, and I was left stretched out full-length on the incline, holding onto the rope. But all was not lost. Right before I let go of the rope and slid back down into the hole, Minnie saw her golden opportunity and ran up my back as if it were a ladder. When she got to the top of my head, she planted her front feet firmly in my scalp and with a mighty leap, was out of the cellar hole! After I slid back to the bottom, I looked up to see Minnie and Sidney peering down at me. I could have sworn I heard Minnie say, "Ta-Dummm!"

So, back to square one. . . . Well, not exactly square one. After all, Minnie was out.

I called to Len to send Jim to the toolshed for the hatchet so I could chop some footholds in the ice. But he said that there was an electric cable buried someplace in the vicinity of the incline and I would light myself up like a Christmas tree if I hit it. So much for *that* idea.

Then Len found the answer: "I'll call the neighbors at the end of the road and see if they can come and pull you out with their pick-up truck!"

"No way!" I yelled. "I'll stay in this hole till spring before I'll let somebody I don't even know come down here and pull me out with a truck, like some old cow in a mud bog!"

"Do you know how long it is until spring?" he asked.

"Just lower me down a bucket of chicken noodle soup," I said in the most wistful, frozen martyr's voice I could muster.

Then, as if the thought of hot soup thawed out my brain a bit, I remembered something. Before I picked up Len at the hospital, I had stopped at the feed store and bought a twenty-pound bag of salt to sprinkle on the ground between the barn and our trailer house so I could walk without falling. But Len had said that when the ground thawed out, the salt could work its way down into our water supply. At this point, though, the water supply was the last thing on my mind.

The salt was still in the truck where Len couldn't get to it. Jim was too small to lift it, but Len gave him a bucket and had him go out there and scoop salt out of the bag and into the bucket. Then Jim stood at the top of the cellar hole and threw handfuls of salt all over the incline. I waited a few minutes and then ... Ta-Dummm!

Jesus said that we are the "salt of the earth." We give a flavor to life that can help make it a little more palatable. Maybe, just maybe, we're also salt on a frozen uphill path that someone is trying to climb. I like to think of it like that.

Don't Look Now ...

Whon my son was in the second grade, I went as a parent sponsor to the zoo with his class. It was one of many zoo trips I'd make before my kids got into the higher grades. In fact, I went on so many school "zoo trips" that I got the feeling the animals were beginning to recognize me. They looked at me as if they were saying, "Look, there's that woman again. Why doesn't she get a life?"

There was a shortage of parent sponsors for the trip that year, and when I told the teacher I wasn't going to be able to go, either, since I couldn't find a baby-sitter for Chris, she laughed and said, "You are such a kidder."

I didn't have the heart to tell her I wasn't kidding. Besides, I started thinking that maybe if there was such a sponsor shortage, my son could possibly get separated from the group and maybe get left at the zoo, where he would wander around aimlessly until he was finally adopted by the apes. Then I would only get to see him when I would go on school trips with Chris's class after she started school. I would take him bananas and sing the *Speed Racer* theme song to him, hoping to touch some hidden memory. But it probably wouldn't work, and he would grow up with the apes and eventually get married. All of my grandchildren would have long arms and hair behind their ears.

So you do what you have to do, and I had to go to the zoo with my eighteen-month-old daughter and twenty-four second graders.

The first two hours weren't bad—Chris enjoyed riding in the stroller. But then she got tired and wanted me to carry her. This arrangement worked fine—for her. As for me, by the time we got to the gorilla compound, I was worn out.

I was standing with my weight on one foot, holding Chris on my hip, as I watched the gorillas on the other side of the glass. Suddenly, I felt as though I was being watched. Looking toward the far end of the enclosure, I discovered why I had that feeling. There was a mama gorilla standing with her weight on one foot, holding her baby on her hip. She kept looking at me and then at Chris. For a second, I wasn't exactly sure just who was in the zoo. It seemed very possible that the gorillas had decided to move into that neighborhood because they had heard that human beings could often be observed passing through on their way to feed at the "pizza pits."

As we stood there watching each other, it seemed as if we shared a common bond . . . frazzled motherhood.

For whatever reason, her baby didn't seem to want to be put down. Maybe it was teething or just plain fussy. At any rate, that mama gorilla looked as tired as I felt.

She stood there with her baby on her hip, looking at me with my baby on my hip, my face all red and my hair sticking out in a dozen directions. She had to be wondering why in the world I didn't go home. She had seen me there before, and it seemed to her that anyone with as many kids as I had (and she had seen me with at least two dozen of them) should be able to find *something* to do at home.

Finally, after watching me for a couple of minutes, she abruptly turned her back to us. Her baby was looking up at her as though it were listening to something she was telling it.

I imagined she was saying, "Someday you will probably hear about something called 'Darwin's theory of evolution' ... don't you believe it for one minute!"

"So God created man in his own image, in the image of God he created him; male and female he created them" (Genesis 1:27).

Say What?

The summer after I graduated from high school, I went to Virginia with my aunt to visit her family. They lived in a small town that was built on the side of a mountain. In the evening, the side of that mountain looked like a Christmas tree with the lights shining from all of the houses and smoke coming from the chimneys. It was like visiting a calendar picture. Even now, when I see a picturesque scene on a calendar, I have a tendency to look closer to see if I can spot someone I know.

With the town built on the side of the mountain like that, it seemed like we were always walking either up or down. By the time we got back to Oklahoma, I was so used to leaning either forward or backward that I had almost forgotten how to walk straight.

I really liked the people there. Of course, my being from Oklahoma, they thought I talked funny. On the other hand, my being from Oklahoma, I thought *they* talked funny.

In Oklahoma, if we want to say we're going someplace, we might say, "I'm gonna run over to . . . ." In Virginia they would say, "I'm goin' down the road to . . . ." And there was another expression that the older people used that I just loved. If someone were out on a date, they would say, "They've gone out sparkin'."

So while I thought "goin' down the road" was funny, they thought "gonna run over" was funny. Someone from New York would think we all sounded funny. But, then again, a New York accent would stick out like a sore thumb in Oklahoma or Virginia.

What it all boils down to is that it doesn't matter so much *what* you say; people pay more attention to *how* you say it. And that can be disastrous especially if you happen to be on a bicycle when you're not paying attention to the content of the message.

The house where we were staying was about halfway down the mountain, and when I say "down," I mean DOWN! That road in front of their house was as straight down as any road I've ever seen, and much straighter down than I ever want to see again—especially from the seat of a bicycle with no brakes.

Everyone was in the house having lunch. I was already finished eating and was sitting on the porch swing when I noticed the bike lying in the front yard.

You know that little lightbulb that flashes on in your head when you have an idea? Well, I saw that bike, and the bulb came on. I found myself thinking what a wonderful way to burn off some of the calories I had just stored away on my hips for future use! (Sometimes I think it would be to my benefit to unscrew that bulb before it ever has a chance to bring some ideas to light.)

I stood the bicycle up and looked at it for a minute. It had been a while since I had ridden one of those things, but they obviously still had two wheels, handlebars, and a seat— what more could I ask for? Maybe some brakes?

I got on and pedaled around the yard once. Confirming to myself that I hadn't lost the magic formula for one of those machines, I turned out of the driveway and headed down the mountain. I didn't have in mind to go very far because I knew that since the road was so steep, I'd have to push the bike back.

As I turned out of the driveway, my aunt's nephew ran out onto the porch, yelling and waving his arms. The only words I managed to catch were "down" and "road." We had been teasing each other so much about our accents that I thought he was just joking around again.

"Yeah, I'm gonna run down the road," I said, laughing at my own play on words.

Well, "run down the road" wasn't exactly what I did. I FLEW down the road. In fact, it seems I remember seeing faces peering at me from the windows of a jumbo jet as I passed.

As I pedaled out onto the road, I coasted for a few seconds before casually applying what I thought would be the brakes. But instead of finding brakes, I found nothing but air.

At that point, I was already moving along at a pretty good clip. Instead of putting my foot down and dragging to a stop, I wasted more precious seconds backpedaling. It all happened so fast, I think my reflexes kicked in and began babbling panicky instructions to me like, "Keep pedaling backward, those brakes have got to be someplace!" I searched for them for a few more seconds, but in those few seconds that bike picked up a lot more speed.

The road was paved; I hate to think about going that fast on gravel. On the left, the road was held in check by the mountain that went straight up. On the right, it dropped straight down several hundred feet. You've heard that expression, "Watch that first step, it's a dilly ..."

In life-threatening situations, they say, your whole life passes in front of you. I only reviewed the last thirty minutes. I was thinking that if I had known I was going to be in this kind of mess, I'd have gone ahead and had seconds on dessert. Besides, if I'd had seconds, I'd still be sitting in the kitchen instead of breaking the sound barrier and whatever else I was fixing to break on the road.

By now, I was dragging one foot on the pavement in an effort to slow down to at least the speed of light. You know that eventually I did come to a stop, or I wouldn't be sitting here right now writing my "memoirs." I'd still be airborne someplace over the picturesque state of Virginia. People could locate me on calendar pictures. I'd be the one that was silhouetted against the moon, still in the riding position on that bicycle.

Now, there have been some exaggerations here. I didn't really pass a jet plane, and I probably wasn't going quite as fast as the speed of light, but I'll tell you two things that are not exaggerated.

One is how scared I was. I wasn't afraid or frightened—those are wimpy feelings! I was S-C-A-R-E-D—SCARED!!! A person is "frightened" when she sees a mouse. WIMPY! Or someone may be "afraid" of the dark because the dark represents the unknown. You don't know what's waiting for you in the dark. But I knew what was waiting for me as I looked down at the tops of trees speeding by on the right-hand side of the road, and I was **SCARED**!

The second thing that is not exaggerated is what happened to my shoe. I was holding onto that bike for dear life as my foot dragged the pavement. I could feel a faint sensation of heat on the bottom of my foot, but I really didn't have time to even wonder what it was. When I finally did get that bike stopped, I half-climbed and half-fell off of it. After allowing myself the luxury of feeling good ol' terra firma standing still under my feet, I began the long walk back up the mountain. That was when I felt something rough on the bottom of my foot. I looked and discovered that the pavement had burned a hole completely through the sole of my shoe! I'd been wearing loafers. I think if I'd been wearing tennis shoes, there wouldn't have been enough "give" between the pavement and the shoes and it would have thrown me and the bike into the wild blue yonder.

I'm glad that even though I wasn't riding a bicycle built for two, the Lord was riding with me down that mountain anyhow! Besides, I think mountains are one of God's specialties.

Sink or Swim

Some people are destined to sleep on waterbeds, lulled into a peaceful slumber by the gentle movement of water. My husband and I obviously are not in that group of seafaring dreamers. We have been awakened by the gentle movement of water when the kids were small and would wake up in the night, invite themselves into our bed, and then peacefully sleep through Mother Nature's call.

Len and I did go the waterbed route for a couple of years, and it was wonderful for a while. We had a king-sized, semi-waveless bed so that there was a slight, gentle rocking motion—not enough to get seasick, but enough to be able to smell the salt air if you closed your eyes. Or, as in one case, after closing my eyes, I thought I could detect a fishy smell like the one you find around a lake sometimes. About the time I decided to get my fishing pole and check that mattress out, I discovered that one of the kids had stuck a partially eaten tuna sandwich in the side of the mattress.

It was kind of a disappointment. I love to fish more than almost anything. I can get one whiff of a good, fishy-smelling lake and my pulse quickens, my eyes start to twitch, and I have to get a line in the water really quickly or I start incoherently babbling old fish stories. By the time I found the sandwich, I was already so worked up into a fishing frenzy that I gave some serious thought to having that sandwich mounted on a plaque for the bedroom wall.

As comfortable as that waterbed was, it was doomed from the start. I don't know who invented the waterbed, but I do know they didn't have kids or cats. We had both. In all fairness to the kids, they weren't so hard on the waterbed (except, of course, that one incident with Jim's dart gun, and a few times when Chris used it for a trampoline when I wasn't looking).

The cats were the big problem. We couldn't have them declawed because they spent quite a bit of time outside where they needed those claws. (It's too bad somebody can't invent little miniature claws that could be strapped onto the feet of declawed cats when they go outside.)

Of course, the cats weren't allowed in our bedroom, much less on the bed. Right! Cats are so quiet and so quick, but mostly they are so sneaky. Keeping those cats out of there was like keeping a fly in a birdcage.

Consequently, we had patch after patch after patch—until finally, the patches started needing patches. Now, patching always took care of the problem, but I had a thick mattress pad on that bed, and sometimes the cats would make a very subtle little "alteration" in the mattress. It would leak for a few days before it soaked through and was noticed.

Sometimes, the mattress would begin to get a little bit "low tide," and I would just add another patch and make a mental note to myself to "water" that bed in a day or two or the first chance I got—whichever came first.

As the "day or twos" began to stretch into three or four and the three or fours into five or sixes, that waterbed soon began to feel the stress of modern-day living until one night, it just gave up and burst.

It happened in the middle of the night while Len and I were sound asleep. When it burst, my posterior landed on the heating coil which had somehow, in all that rush of water, come out of the protective covering. If you want to wake up in a hurry, try sitting on one of those things! It works better than coffee.

I rolled off of the hot spot in a flash, and as I did, I discovered I was up to my chin in water. The first thought I had was that we were going to be electrocuted, but evidently preventive measures have been taken to keep that from happening in that situation.

Shaking Len, who was still snoring away even though he was up to his ears in water, I said, "Len, wake up! The waterbed burst!"

Without even opening his eyes, and barely interrupting the rhythm of his snores, he said, "It's not leaking on my side."

Up until then, I never knew anyone who could tread water in his sleep.

By that time I thought I could faintly hear the theme song from *Jaws* and could have sworn I saw a fin circling us in the murky water that had once been our bed.

"LEN, WAKE UP! THE WATERBED BURST!!!" I yelled again.

This time he opened his eyes and just lay there a few seconds with no expression on his face at all. But as the truth began to, literally, soak in, his eyes got big, and he started splashing and clawing his way out of the sinking bed.

Fortunately, we both managed to get out without any help from the Coast Guard, but I have never seen so much water in my whole life! I think the *Titanic* could have sunk in our bedroom that night.

We didn't replace the waterbed with another one. We decided that our lifestyle was better suited for more conventional sleeping arrangements. And besides, after that night, I don't think I could sleep in a waterbed without wearing a life jacket, and those things are so uncomfortable to sleep in.

The Writing's on the Wall

When God was checking the husband situation out for me, He knew I would need someone with enough patience to put up with me, and adequate gumption to say when enough was enough. And when God does something, He never does it halfway. When Len is being patient, he is very, very patient, but when he is not—he is NOT! When he has had enough, he has gumption coming out of his ears!

When he's being impatient, there is no doubt at all that you are seeing impatience, but when he's exercising gumption, sometimes it comes in a different form than the dictionary's definition of the word. The dictionary refers to it as "courage," "initiative," and "enterprise." After twenty-five years of marriage to Len, my definition of gumption is—solid—as in "brick wall." Because when he reaches the point of needing to use his gumption, I can talk until I'm red, white, and blue, and I might as well be talking to a brick wall. He is just that immovable, too.

An example of this happened when I was expecting our second baby. My parents were coming from Dallas to visit for a few days, and I desperately wanted our bathroom painted. It was sort of sea-sick green. In fact, that color was so bad that before I found out I was pregnant, I didn't realize I was having morning sickness. I just thought it was my normal reaction to that color.

My parents had seen that bathroom before, so it really wasn't any big deal, but I thought maybe I could coerce Len into painting it if I used their coming as an excuse. I couldn't paint it in my "delicate" condition on account of the fumes, so let the games begin!

I asked him. He said he would, and time passed. I begged him. He said he would, and time passed. I pleaded, cajoled, and pouted. He said he would and time...

Finally, a friend told me about a book she had read where this lady kept begging her husband to paint a certain room and he kept putting it off, so she took a bright-colored paint and painted messages all over the wall, forcing him to paint the room.

Now, before I go any further with this story, let me put a word of caution here: Do Not Try This at Home! Believe me, it looks better on paper.

I don't know if being pregnant affected my mind, or if I simply had a temporary bout of insanity—kind of like the stomach flu or something, but one day while Len was at work, I took a red, permanent-ink laundry marker and painted messages all over the bathroom wall.

The messages said things like: "This wall needs paint!"; "So does this wall!"; "Needs some here, too!"; and "Try a dollop here!"

The walls were painted with flat paint and if that marker hadn't already been the permanent kind, it would have become permanent when it hit that flat green!

Len came home from work all tired and hot and not really in the right frame of mind to see the humor in my little "joke." They say that timing is everything in humor—well, my timing was way off that day. So was Len's sense of humor, for that matter. In fact, if he even had a sense of humor that particular afternoon it was disguised as "grouchy."

When he walked through the front door and I saw his face, my temporary insanity disappeared, and the one word that popped into my mind was *Oops!* But when you've put permanent red on flat green, "Oops" is a little bit lame.

Hoping to help him understand why I had done what he was about to see, I opened my mouth and heard myself say, "Hi." I waited to hear myself say more, but it seemed that my tongue had shorted out. It would speak, but nothing over two words. Anything more and it shut down.

"Hi," he answered. "Boy, this has been a rotten day. Everything that could possibly go wrong went wrong at the plant. I'm glad to be home."

"Oh, rats," I said.

"Rats? Is that 'rats' because I'm home, or 'rats' because you've had a bad day, too?"

"Well, being pregnant—," I ventured, managing three words this time. Maybe I could convince him that insanity temporarily showed up in all of the pregnant women in my family.

"Is supper ready?" he asked, tuning out my pregnancy woes.

"Yes," I said, reverting back to one word again.

"Okay, let me wash up and we can compare days while we eat. I'm starved!" he said as he headed toward THE ROOM OF DOOM!

He disappeared down the hall, leaving me to contemplate my fate in terms of one-word sentences.

How could I have done something that dumb? If I could freeze-frame a moment in time and then go back and take that frame out, it would be when I took that marker in my hand and began doing my dastardly deed.

About two minutes later Len appeared in the doorway of the kitchen. He just stood there, staring at me like I had lost my mind. The message I was getting was that he surely must be thinking, *Insanity must run in the pregnant women in her family.*

Well, he wasn't real happy with me. What he said was the same thing he said when I first asked him to paint the bathroom: "I'll do it." And time passed.

However, this time he really did get it painted, but he didn't do it until the day before they came. Guess he thought he'd make me sweat a little.

There is a bittersweet postscript to this. The night before my folks came, he painted the bathroom white and beautiful, but the next morning when we got up, we discovered that the red marker had bled through the white paint. There were all of these little pink messages on the bathroom wall.

Now his gumption kicked in. I thought he would be at least a little ruffled, but he wasn't. He just went to the kitchen, poured himself a cup of coffee and sat sipping it as if all was well on the Western front.

"Honey, I'm really sorry," I said in my most contrite tone of voice.

"It's no problem. A second coat will cover it okay. It won't be hard to do. I'll get right on it—next week," he said, taking another sip of coffee. "Good coffee," he added.

Brick wall.

I was hoping my folks wouldn't notice the "writing on the wall," but no such luck. The first time my mother came out of the room, she said, "Has Jimmy been writing on the walls in the bathroom?"

For a fleeting second, I was tempted to go ahead and credit the art work to my young son, but Len was standing by to see that I didn't sully Jim's artistic reputation.

"Nah," he said. "Jim does all of his writing in cursive. Connie did that."

After my folks went back home, Len repainted the bathroom, and I threw my laundry marker in the trash.

Of all the husbands that God could have given me, I'm glad He gave me one with gumption. It really keeps me on my toes.

Have you ever thought how much like those walls we can be? I used those walls to write a message to my husband. God uses our lives to write a message to the world.

We show that we are a "letter from Christ, . . . written not with ink but with the Spirit of the living God, not on tablets of stone but on tablets of human hearts" (2 Corinthians 3:3).

Put My Best Foot Where?

Have you ever noticed that when you try the hardest to put your best foot forward, that's when you're most likely to fall flat on your face? Sometimes literally.

Maybe it's a problem of trying to remember which foot it was that we decided was our best one. I don't know, but I do know that the results of accidentally putting our worst foot forward can be embarrassing—even worse than embarrassing when it involves a job interview.

I hate job interviews. When you're being interviewed for a job, you're definitely in *their* territory. They have a job, a paycheck, and company benefits. You have a résumé, a car that's eligible for Social Security, and sweaty palms. And all the time you're sweating bullets you're supposed to look calm, cool, and collected. You're supposed to have an air about you that says to them, "I might consider this job if the pay is right and there's room to go to the top."

If you manage to somehow exude self-confidence, then you know you'll leave that place with a company car and keys to the executive lounge. Right!

What happens if your best foot doesn't cooperate? That happens sometimes. Or maybe you just get beaned over the head by circumstances beyond your control. That happens sometimes, too.

I remember one time when circumstances not only "beaned" me on an interview, they totally shredded my dignity. Fortunately, dignity is kind of like toenails—if you cut one too short, it gets sore and you hobble around a few days, but it does eventually grow back.

I had an appointment for an interview for a job taking pictures for passports. I really needed that job. Besides, I thought it would be fun to take pictures of people who were going someplace interesting. I could sort of vicariously enjoy being a world traveler.

The ad had said they needed someone who was intelligent, personable, and well groomed. So I thought, *Well, two out of three . . .* No, I didn't actually think that at the time I called for an appointment. I *felt* intelligent, personable, and well groomed.

What happened between making the appointment on Thursday and keeping it on Friday was a migraine headache.

I'd been having trouble with them from time to time, and the doctor had given me a new prescription for pain pills that I had never used before. I had never had anything with codeine in it, and I didn't know at the time that I was allergic to that stuff.

Thursday night I developed a whopper of a headache. So I took a pill and went to bed. I woke up later, feeling much worse, so I took another one. I've searched my dictionary of synonyms for a delicate way to write "throwing up," and I really can't find one. But that's what I did all night.

My appointment was at nine the next morning. I should have canceled it, but I really wanted that job. Now at that point, I realized I didn't feel intelligent, personable, and well groomed, but those people would surely know that I am usually intelligent, personable, and well groomed. Besides, that job was MINE! It was my destiny to take pictures of people who were going out into the world, clutching passports with "pictures by Connie" (I would be so good that they, naturally, would have me sign my name by each picture).

The studio was located right in the middle of downtown Dallas. I lived about thirty minutes from there.

First of all, when I left that morning, I was about the color of unbaked pie crust. My eyes had dark circles under them and looked like they were sunk about five inches into my head. If I had been applying for a zombie job in a movie I'd have had it made.

The second whack that fate gave me was that about halfway into Dallas the sky opened up and it began raining like—I would say, cats and dogs, but it was even worse than that. By the time I got to town, it was still coming down in a torrential downpour. I didn't have even so much as a newspaper to put over my head, and I couldn't find a parking place. I had to park in a parking lot that was nearly two blocks from my job interview.

Do you think I chickened out? Are you kidding? These people needed my expertise. When I walked through that door, they would breathe a sigh of relief to know that their search for the right person for the job was over!

When I *did* walk through that door, my hair was plastered to my head like a wet mop. My mascara was running down my face in two little, black trails. My dress, which had a full skirt, was totally soaked and was hanging on me like a limp blanket. There was something else I didn't discover until I got home. As if to add insult to injury, the hem had come out of the back of my dress.

So there I stood, pasty-faced, hollow-eyed, stringy-haired, and not looking totally fashion-conscious at that moment. You've heard that expression "She got on the bandwagon"? Well, I looked like I had just been run over by one.

The man behind the counter couldn't imagine anyone's coming down there like that to get their picture taken, but it certainly never entered his mind that I had come there looking like that for a job interview.

"Can I help you?" he asked, not really believing that he or anybody else could help me.

"Yes, I have an appointment for a job interview," I said, as I attempted to smooth back my already plastered-down hair.

He just looked at me as though he wasn't sure he had heard correctly. "A job interview?" he asked.

"Yes," I said in the most intelligent tone of voice I could muster at the time.

I thought about trying to explain my circumstances, but I decided that would probably just make it worse. Besides, maybe if I didn't call attention to my state of being, they wouldn't notice.

"Uh, yes, just a minute, let me get—uh—our—," he said as he disappeared into the next room.

He reappeared with an application form and told me to have a seat and fill it out.

It didn't take very long. When I gave it back to him, he glanced at it as more of a matter of courtesy than interest and told me they would file my application with the others and would call if they decided to hire me.

By then I knew I had flubbed. I knew where they were going to "file" my application. By the time I got around the corner, the only evidence they'd have that I had been there at all would be the wet spot I left on the couch where I had been sitting.

So I didn't get the job. I told myself at the time that it was a shame, because who knows, I might have done wonders taking passport pictures. People might have started having passport pictures framed, they'd be so good.

As it turned out, it was the best thing to happen to me. After that, I got a job at a factory where I met my future sister-in-law, who introduced me to my future husband. Now *that's* what I would call a perfect picture!

I'm glad that we don't have to worry about putting our best foot forward to impress God—Jesus already did that for us. Now, when God looks at us, He sees us as personable, intelligent, and "well groomed."

"But you were washed, you were sanctified, you were justified in the name of the Lord Jesus Christ and by the spirit of our God" (1 Corinthians 6:11).

Bottom Heavy

The summer I was nine years old, my mother made a bathing suit for me out of pink-and-white flowered, polished cotton. Did I feel gorgeous, or what?

I had a white bathing cap to match. Remember those? If you do, then you remember how they fit so tightly that they made wrinkles across your forehead. And when you stuffed your hair up inside the cap, it pulled and hurt. But a wrinkled face and a lumpy head didn't matter to me—I matched and I felt beautiful.

I was about to launch into my second summer of swimming lessons. I had completed the beginners' class and had been promoted for the next year into the intermediate class.

It was the first lesson of the summer, and I couldn't wait to show off my matching outfit. As I walked out of the dressing room and across to the pool, I thought I could hear all of the other little girls ooohing and ahhhing. And I expected at least one little boy to stick his foot out and trip me as a token of his hidden adoration.

But not wanting to appear aware of my stylish entrance, I pretended to be concentrating very intently on finding the pool. I'm sure this only served to deepen the wrinkles in my forehead and made the other kids wonder if I was going to fall outright into the pool before I located it.

Since it was the first day, we each had to swim across the deep end of the pool to assure the instructor that we hadn't forgotten what we had learned the summer before.

When it was my turn, I jumped in and immediately bobbed to the surface and began sort of a combination of the breaststroke and the dog paddle. I felt just like Esther Williams. Maybe when I got to the middle of the pool I should have dived under the water, leaving just my feet showing above the surface with my toes pointing to the sky, just as I had seen Esther do in the movies. After all, I was dressed for the occasion.

I got to the middle and, sure enough, I began my descent under the water. But not quite the way I had thought about. In the first place, I had only been thinking about it, as I might think about swinging from vine to vine with Tarzan. I wasn't ready for synchronized swimming any more than I was ready to swing from vine to vine with anybody, including the King of the Jungle.

About halfway across the pool I seemed to be getting heavier in my bottom section. It was as if I were gaining instant weight. It got harder and harder to keep my head above the surface until, finally, I was beating that water, ninety to nothing, with both hands. If I'd been a frog in a milk can, thrashing around like that, it wouldn't have taken long and I'd have had a pat of butter to climb out on.

But not being a frog in a jug of milk, I had to depend on other resources, and there one was, right in my face. It was the long pole Mr. Maxton, our instructor, used to pull floundering swimmers out of deep water. Was I glad to see that pole!

I grabbed it with both hands and held on while Mr. Maxton pulled me back to the side of the pool.

"What happened to you? You were doing great at the start," he said.

"I don't know," I said as I struggled up the ladder and out of the water. It really took some effort to climb out of the pool, but I thought it was just because I was tired.

I adjusted my suit, pulling the top up and the bottom down, and when I tugged the legs, water poured out like a mini Niagara Falls. Mr. Maxton didn't notice the water, and I didn't know it hurt anything. After all, it was a bathing suit, and I had been in the pool ...

Mother had made my suit with sort of a short-bloomer effect on the bottom with elastic in the legs. That polished cotton was holding more water in those bloomers than a camel could carry.

"Well, try again," Mr. Maxton said.

"Okay," I answered, wishing now that the spotlight was back in Hollywood on Esther Williams instead of on me. This could get embarrassing.

I jumped in and began swimming across the pool. Fine, fine, keep swimming, everything's working—I'm swimming, I'm swimming—I'm sinking! I'm sinking! The pole! Where's the pole! My hand found the pole and once again I was being towed in like a fish.

"Connie, you're panicking! Don't panic! You start out like a swimmer and end up like an egg beater! Don't do that!" Mr. Maxton said in a rather loud tone of voice.

Was my instructor getting frustrated? Well, if he wanted to know what frustration is, he should be on the other end of that pole! I didn't know what the problem was. All I knew was that I could swim halfway across the pool before some invisible hand started pulling me under. Then I had to get towed in while the other kids were laughing their heads off! That, Mr. Maxton, was frustration.

"Try again," he said, his impatience beginning to float to the top.

"Okay," I said, as I adjusted my suit, letting the water gush out.

This time I held my nose with one hand when I jumped in. I had never seen Miss Williams do that before, but I'm sure she had her problems; I sure had mine. And at that point, I had already taken in more water through my nose than I thought the whole pool held.

I went through the entire process all over again. Swim halfway across, thrash around, start to sink, and get towed in.

"Try again!" he shouted.

I tried again—same results.

This time Mr. Maxton did the unpardonable: He banished me to the shallow end of the pool to practice with the beginners!

Me! With my new pink-and-white flowered bathing suit with the matching white bathing cap! How could he do that? I couldn't imagine Esther Williams in the shallow end, holding on to the side of the pool doing splash kicks with the beginners. Not with the gorgeous suits *she* wore!

Not only that, Mr. Maxton called my mother that evening and told her I needed to be put back into the beginners' class.

Without ever having heard the word *humiliating,* I discovered that day what it meant.

"I don't want to take swimming lessons," I told Mother.

"Of course you do," she said. "You've got to learn how to swim. By the way, how do you like your new bathing suit?"

Didn't grown-ups ever listen?

"I like my new bathing suit, except I have to let the water out of it when I get out of the pool. But I don't want to take swimming lessons anymore!"

Mother stood staring at me until I was totally uncomfortable.

Whoops, I thought. Maybe I did want to take swimming lessons after all.

"You mean that bathing suit holds water?" she said.

"Yes, but I let it out," I answered.

She started laughing. Grown-ups are hard to figure out.

She made a phone call to Mr. Maxton who then agreed to give me another chance in the intermediate class.

The next morning, Mother and I went to town to buy me another bathing suit. It wasn't as flashy as my "Esther Williams" one, but it worked. And I got to keep my bathing cap.

That afternoon at swimming class when it was my turn to go across the pool, I took a deep breath, jumped in, and swam as hard as I could until I got to the middle. Then ... I kept on swimming! Esther would have been proud!

I'm continually amazed at how many times God pulls us out of deep water. In Ephesians 6:11, we're told to put on the full armor of God. If we do that then we can swim right through the deep water without getting so much as one noseful of H_2O. It's when we put our "bloomers" on that we have trouble keeping our heads above water.

Those bloomers can be made out of many different things—guilt, pride, anger, envy—there's definitely no shortage of bloomer material.

I'm glad that our bloomers are homemade. I'd hate to think that God would weigh us down with an outfit like that.

I'm also glad that even when we do weigh ourselves down, God always pulls us out. We may get a noseful of water, but He always pulls us out!

A Worm Is a Worm, and by Any Other Name . . .

People have been selling the Brooklyn Bridge for as long as there have been people willing to buy it. In fact, that's about the world's oldest joke. But a few years ago some people really *did* buy the London Bridge, and not only did they buy it, they had it moved to Arizona where they now make a fortune charging people to look at it.

Can you imagine how somebody feels right now after having turned down a chance to buy the Brooklyn Bridge at one time or another? He is probably telling himself, "Oh, man, I lost a great opportunity!" But he shouldn't feel too bad. There are plenty more opportunities around like that. There's always someone, someplace who is willing to sell you the Grand Canyon or the Statue of Liberty or, if you really get lucky, the Milky Way!

If the rewards seem lucrative enough and the "con man" is slick enough, people can be convinced of anything—look what Satan persuaded Eve to do. Talk about a con job— we're *still* paying for that one!

Len and I lucked out one time and got in on the ground floor of a great moneymaking deal. This deal actually did work. People really did make money with it. The problem was, it was other people and our money.

Len came home one day, excited about an opportunity one of the guys at work had told him about. For only three hundred fifty dollars we could buy a worm ranch!

We had both always talked about owning a ranch. Here was our chance—and for a mere three hundred fifty dollars! Was that kismet or what?

While Len was stationed overseas right after we were married, I received a very official-looking document from Washington. It was a copy of our brand that Len had registered and was on file at our nation's capital.

This man was serious about someday owning a ranch. We were now the proud owners of our own official brand, and we didn't have even so much as a chicken to put it on.

Our brand was an "L" with a "C" kind of sitting on its lap. I thought it was cute, and over the years I imagined that brand on everything—except on a worm.

"A worm ranch?" I said, trying to envision what branding time would be like.

"Yeah, there's this pet food company in Texas that makes pet food out of freeze-dried worms. They'll buy all of the worms that we can grow!" he said.

"Do we have to freeze them?" I asked, already feeling a little squeamish.

"No! We just raise them and, after about a year, we contact the company, and they'll send us a little harvesting contraption that sorts the worms into different sizes. Then we ship them in boxes with special worm bedding. The company does the rest. All that'll be left for us to do is deposit our check and start on the next year's crop of worms."

The dollar signs in his eyes reflected so brightly in my face that I was suddenly overcome with a hankering to be a rancher's wife!

"Well, yippi-ki-yo! Let's do it!" I answered, blinking in the sudden light brought on by the dollar signs now shining in my own eyes.

Now there were several things that should have alerted us to the possibility that this was a fraud. For one thing, why would they want the worms separated into different sizes if they were just going to be made into pet food? Well, maybe the final product would come in small, medium and large sizes for Chihuahuas, cocker spaniels, and St. Bernards.

The other thing that made this deal seem a little suspicious was the actual harvesting contraption itself. How in the world would a machine go about sizing live worms?

I did ask Len about that, and he said the "harvester," as it was called, was some kind of machine with different-sized holes in it, and it just separated the different-sized worms into the holes.

"How are we supposed to make the worms crawl through the right holes?" I asked, trying to imagine all of those worms standing in line for hours, waiting their turn to crawl through the right hole.

"I don't know," he said with an edge of impatience to his voice. "They said that when the time comes they'll send a man down with the harvester to show us how to do it. In the meantime, all we have to do is grow the worms."

Len had a brochure with the phone number on it. We called, and they were very nice on the phone and seemed to think we would make first-class worm ranchers. They were so nice, in fact, that I wondered if they had a list from Washington with all of the names of people who actually had brands officially on file. After all, that would definitely be a sign that we were serious ranch-type people.

This first thing we had to do was mail the three hundred fifty dollars. This would not only buy everything we needed for a worm ranch, it would buy the worms, too. But there was more—it also paid our dues for an entire year for the National Worm Ranchers Association. Just think, we'd be members in good standing of the N.W.R.A.! That was what I'd call "uptown"! Of course, we had never heard of the N.W.R.A. before, but then again, we had never been worm ranchers, either.

We mailed the money and then waited impatiently for our "ranch" to arrive. About two weeks later, it came. It wasn't exactly what we were expecting, but it came. It was a box about the size of a shoe box, and it was full of worms.

I really don't know what we expected them to send. You don't use horses on a worm ranch and you don't need a chuck wagon or ranch hands—you just need worms. And they sent worms.

"Honey, these look like plain old worms to me," I said, thinking that N.W.R.A. worms should look at least a little different.

"Yeah, they kind of do," he said, "But these worms are registered with the N.W.R.A., so they've probably been bred for a higher protein level."

Sounded good to me.

We were now actual worm ranchers—step aside, Ponderosa!

Len built two worm beds. Each bed was about eight feet long and three feet wide. We filled them full of special bedding we got at a greenhouse, divided the worms into the two beds, covered the beds with carpet remnants, and began "life on the ranch."

We bought meal at the feed store, and every day we pulled the carpet back and sprinkled meal over the beds, covered them again and then wet the carpet down with the water hose. The worms loved their ranch house.

Like any working "ranch," we had a few problems. The biggest one for me was that a lot of time when I pulled the carpet back, there'd be a snake curled up under it. I hated that! I'd use a rake to pull the carpet, and if there was a snake I'd get back until it had time to get out of there. They were just old garden snakes, but still. . . .

Well, we "ranched" for a year, and by the time the year was over you wouldn't believe how many worms were living in those beds. Worms are more prolific than rabbits!

Once again, Len called the people at the N.W.R.A. They didn't seem surprised that we had been so successful. (Yep, they really must have checked with Washington.)

They said that they were just fixing to contact us anyway because it was time for us to pay our fifty dollars that would be due once a year to renew our membership in the N.W.R.A. They told us that as soon as they got the dues, the man would be down with the harvester.

We sent the dues. Two weeks went by, no word. Two more weeks—nothing. Two more—still nothing. By this time, Len and I both were beginning to get a bad feeling about the situation, but neither of us said anything to the other.

Another week passed and Len said, "I'm going to call those guys. There's something wrong."

"Maybe the envelope with the dues in it got lost in the mail," I ventured.

"Maybe," he said, "but I don't think so."

He finished dialing. He waited a minute, then he put the receiver back on the phone and turned around. The look on his face explained it.

"The phone has been disconnected," he said.

We wrote to them, but the letter came back, stamped "No such business at that address."

So ended our ranching career. We lost our money, but the N.W.R.A. lost us. And we were probably the two best worm ranchers they ever had!

Yep! We were conned, all right. But that's okay. It's nice to know we don't have to try to outsmart the biggest con artist in the world: Satan. He promises us the world on a silver platter if we will just go his way. But Jesus knows how Satan is, and He is ready for him. If anybody knows how to take care of the "snake under the carpet," it's the Lord! When Jesus speaks, Satan listens. He may not like it, but he listens.

So Where's the Fire?

When I was growing up, there was a little boy in our neighborhood who, as regular as clockwork, would play with matches and end up setting something on fire—like the alley or his garage and, in one case, his house.

Hearing the sirens blaring toward our neighborhood and then watching the firemen at work was exciting for us little kids. Of course, I'm sure the adults didn't particularly enjoy living in the middle of a potential marshmallow roast all the time.

I remember being sort of amazed by the things he got punished for. All of the kids in the neighborhood got punished by their parents for one thing or another—having rock fights was a favorite, or stealing pears from the neighbor's tree—these were things we got in trouble for. But he went for the big stuff.

Once, after the fire department had been dispatched to the alley behind his house, I saw him gazing wistfully from his bedroom window.

"Come out, and let's play cowboys. You can be Roy Rogers, and I'll be Dale Evans," I said, thinking that no one could turn down a chance to be "King of the Cowboys."

"I can't," he said tearfully. "My mama thinks I caused the fire in the alley."

"Did you?" I asked.

"Not on purpose," he said.

Well, so much for the "King of the Cowboys."

I never started a fire when I was growing up. I waited until I was married and had kids. Then I started a fire!

At the time, Chris was four years old, Jim was at school, Len was at work, and I decided to burn trash.

It was too windy to be burning anything, but we had a big hole up on the hill that we were going to have made into a cellar. It was the second hole we'd had dug for that purpose. The first one had been closer to our trailer house, but we decided to put the cellar in a place that would be closer to the house we planned to build. Had the fire been in the first hole by the trailer, we'd really have had a problem!

I had put a couple of bags of garbage in the hole and lit them. I was standing there with Chris, watching the fire like any dutiful citizen who was burning trash when she shouldn't. Everything was going fine until I noticed a paper sack of what I thought was trash, sitting on the back of Len's old flatbed truck.

After checking it out, I was sure it was trash, so I threw it on the fire. Chris and I were watching as the sack began to burn. As it burned away, I noticed an aerosol can of machine oil that must have been buried way down at the bottom of the sack. The top of the can was burning like the Olympic torch. I wouldn't have been surprised to see a torchbearer come running out of that hole.

But if he had, I'd have passed him as if he were standing still! I scooped up Chris and started running for safer ground.

I ran about fifty feet before I stopped and turned around to look. Just as I turned, that can of oil exploded in a giant, fiery mushroom about thirty feet into the air. I've never seen anything quite like that before, not even at one of Len's Fourth of July celebrations!

When the fire came back down, it completely engulfed the cellar hole. The grass around the hole was high and dry, and that fire took off as if it were alive!

I put Chris in the trailer house and told her to stay put because the wind was blowing away from the trailer. I grabbed a sheet and wet it down with the water hose because the hose wouldn't reach to the top of the hill where the fire was.

By the time I got back up the hill and began beating the fire with the wet sheet, the fire was already way out of control. We live almost at the end of a dead-end road. There are ten acres of woods between us and the last house on the road, and that was where the fire was heading. The people who lived there weren't home. I could just see myself trying to explain to them what had happened to their house. Smoky the Bear himself would have had a hard time with that one!

I ran back to the trailer and called the fire department, but they weren't home. You see, our fire department is a volunteer unit, and when they've gone to a fire, you just have to wait your turn. You have no idea how discouraging it is to get an answering machine when you call the fire department!

"Hi, this is the fire department. We're at a fire right now, but if you will leave your name and number at the sound of the siren, we'll get back to you."

I called my husband at work and told him what was going on. He headed for home, but it's a twenty-minute drive. A great deal can burn in twenty minutes.

I reinforced my instructions for Chris to stay inside. Then I ran back to the fire and tried to beat it out with a shovel and the wet sheet. By then the trees were burning. It looked like a scene from Dante's *Inferno*!

I'd beat the fire with the shovel, then I'd beat it with the wet sheet. Then I'd run out to the road and yell for help, but nobody heard me because nobody on that road was home except me!

Meanwhile, Chris was busy calling for help on the phone. She couldn't read, but she knew her numbers and she was looking in the yellow pages and calling numbers of businesses that looked to her like fire department ads. She called an insurance company that had a picture of a fire in the ad. They told her to stop playing with the phone. Then she called a pipeline supply place that had pictures of oil-well equipment. They took her seriously!

But they misunderstood her, they thought the fire was *in the house*.

"Get out of the house!" the woman yelled.

"My mama won't let me! Somebody come and help, my mama's going to burn up!" She was crying hysterically now.

"Get out of the house!" the woman repeated with even more urgency.

"I CAN'T!" she cried. "Somebody come and help!"

"Look, it doesn't matter what your mother said—get out of that house!" the woman yelled as she, too, began to panic, thinking some little girl was in a burning house.

In the meantime, the fire department (who really didn't have an answering machine) was coming back from the fire they had been putting out and saw the smoke from the fire at our house.

They switched on their sirens as they turned onto our road right behind my husband, who had made that twenty-minute drive in about twelve. Chris heard the sirens and dropped the phone to look out the front door. When she saw the fire trucks coming behind her daddy, she ran back to the telephone.

"It's okay now. My daddy's here, and he brought the fire trucks with him! I've got to go now, I'm not allowed to play with the phone. Bye!" she said, hanging up the receiver.

After it was all over and we were back in the trailer—minus about four acres of trees but not missing anyone's house—the phone rang. It was the pipeline supply reception. She had managed to get Chris's last name and had been calling every Breedlove in the book trying to find out what was going on.

The woman told me about the call Chris had made, and how happy she had been when she heard the sirens in the background. The woman said that Chris had been more excited about her dad's arriving than she was about the fire department's getting there.

You know that saying, "If it's not broken, don't fix it"? Well, when Chris was growing up, I think she interpreted that as, "If Daddy can't fix it, then it's not broken."

Needless to say, I don't burn trash anymore. But that day, before I went out for that fateful appointment with the fire department, I had been making a tape to send to a friend of mine who lived in Kentucky. We had decided that sending tapes to each other would be cheaper than calling and more interesting than letters.

I was telling her on the tape that there really wasn't anything going on that was interesting enough to talk about. Then I told her I was going to go outside to burn trash, and maybe I would think of something to talk about when I came back in.

The next day, when I went back to the tape and heard myself say that, I started laughing and couldn't even finish the tape until a couple of days later. I think it was a delayed reaction to the fire.

At any rate, I never complained about there being nothing to talk about after that. I also believe it'll rain if you wash your car!

Abba is Arabic for "father," but it's a very personal form of the word. It's equivalent to the English word *papa*. In Israel, "abba" is what little kids call their daddy.

When we call God "Abba," we're just calling Him Papa, which, since we are His children, is very appropriate. He's our God, our Father, our "Abba."

The only people who ever call my husband "Daddy" are his children. And he answers them when they say that, because that's who he is to them.

When we call out to "Abba," He answers, because that's who He is to us.

Just as Chris expected her daddy to take care of her, we can expect our "Abba" to take care of us. I like that!

"Because you are sons, God sent the Spirit of his Son into our hearts, the Spirit who calls out, 'Abba, Father.' So you are no longer a slave, but a son; and since you are a son, God has made you also an heir" (Galatians 4:6–7).

A Hair-Raising Experience

Have you ever thought about what it would be like to be able to take a giant cookie cutter and a big piece of cookie dough and simply cut out a plan for your life? Then you'd just put it in the oven and, a few minutes later, take out a beautifully baked, organized, wonderful life for yourself.

Well, to tell the truth, I've burned enough cookie dough in my life to be totally relieved not to have the responsibility of baking a life plan for myself. And there's a lot I could say about being "half-baked," as well.

No, I'll just leave the job of preparing my life's plan to the Master Chef. He wrote the recipe book. Besides, it's His kitchen.

So, if we let God handle the "cooking" for us, does that mean we're going to have a perfect, uneventful, always-wonderful life? Of course not! Eve took care of that when she threw a handful of forbidden fruit into the recipe!

Have you ever heard that expression, "If you can't stand the heat, get out of the kitchen"? Well, that's where the Lord steps in. He takes the heat for us.

When I was twenty-two years old, I had a really unexpected blast of "kitchen heat" that the Lord handled very nicely for me.

It was in the sixties, and the hair-do of the day was the big—and I'm not exaggerating when I say "big"—bouffant style. Women ratted their hair and sprayed it with so much hair spray that they looked as if they had applied a coat of shellac to their heads before they left the house.

All that ratting and spraying began to take its toll on my hair. Then, to make matters worse, I developed an allergy to hair spray, which caused my hair to start coming out in handfuls! But I didn't know that was what was causing it.

I went to a couple of doctors and a skin specialist before the problem was solved, but by then I looked like Yul Brynner! Talk about an unexpected detour in my life's plan, I certainly didn't expect that! But the Lord was right there, taking the heat. He's so good at that and very understanding about how we feel in certain circumstances. I'll tell you right now, when all of that happened, it was really pretty devastating.

What the Lord said to me was, "Look, Connie, it's just hair! You're still here; I'm still here—let's get on with the rest of the plan!"

So we did. And the first thing the plan called for was a good wig!

I had to wear that wig for eight years before my hair grew back thick enough to get along without it. Even then, my hair didn't come back really thick, but I'm still here and He's still here, and the plan is still cooking—because it was just hair.

Wearing that wig for eight years presented a few challenging incidents from time to time. I remember one day I was visiting my aunt and uncle, who lived out in the country. I was enjoying a ride on my cousin's horse, when I decided to take him a little farther down the road. He really didn't want to go, but I showed him who was boss—I thought—and we went.

But after we had gone a half mile or so, he decided he'd had enough foolishness. He went down into a ditch and back up into some people's front yard. They were sitting on the porch watching my display of great horsemanship when that horse ran me under a tree, catching my wig in the branches. Much to the astonishment of the people watching all of this, the wig lifted right off of my head. I felt it go, and, as it lifted up, I grabbed it back onto my head again. Only this time, it was on crooked, so that the bangs were over my right ear. All of this took place in just a split second. In that split second, the horse decided that now it was his turn to show *me* who was boss, and he took off at a dead run for his little corner of the world.

It took us much less time to get back to the barn than it had taken us to get to the tree. When we arrived back in his barnyard, I was clutching his mane with one hand and holding my wig on with the other.

My uncle took one look at us and started laughing.

"Does he know who's boss, now?" he asked.

"Yeah, I think he does," I answered.

The thing that stands out in my mind about that day was the look on the faces of those people sitting on the porch. I guess the thing that stood out in *their* minds was the look on my face. As for the horse, he enjoyed all of it because I think he planned it that way!

And as far as being embarrassed, I thought about it and decided that Absalom never had it so good!

"Now Absalom happened to meet David's men. He was riding his mule, and as the mule went under the thick branches of a large oak, Absalom's head got caught in the tree. He was left hanging in midair, while the mule he was riding kept on going" (2 Samuel 18:9).

What this Country Needs Is a Good Five-Cent Car!

I've been noticing the cars that kids drive these days—they're really driving some uptown vehicles! I don't want to sound like one of those old-timers who starts off every sentence with "Back when I was a kid . . .", but back when I was a kid, it really was very different.

I paid cold, hard cash for the first car I bought, and it was worth every penny of it—five, to be exact. That's right, I paid one nickel for my car. And that's a bargain anytime.

Inflation has made everything "back then" seem bigger, better, and cheaper, but not even inflation can change the car market *that* much. That was probably the only five-cent car to hit the market before or since that time.

My brother was responsible for a rock-bottom price like that. He had a car—and I can't, for the life of me, remember what kind it was, but I remember it was black, it ran, and he was going to take it to the junkyard. I had never owned my own car before, and I couldn't believe anybody would take a perfectly good car like that to the junkyard!

"The junkyard!" I said. "Why don't you sell it?"

"Because nobody is crazy enough to buy a hunk of junk like that," he said.

"I will!" I said, quickly adding up in my mind how much money I had hidden under the things in my sock and underwear drawer ... and in the coffee can in the garage ... and in the shoe box in the back of my closet. My piggy bank was just an empty decoy in case of burglars—they'd never find my fortune spread out the way it was.

If my estimate was right, I had pretty close to seventeen dollars.

"I'll give you fifteen dollars down and ten dollars a month for ten months," I said, hoping he wouldn't realize that he was dealing with a financial wizard who was fixing to take him to the cleaners on that car.

"If a complete stranger has better sense than to buy this car, do you think I'd sell it to my own sister who doesn't?" he asked.

Okay, so he wanted to play hardball. I could handle that.

"I'll give you fifteen down and fifteen a month for ten months, and that's my last offer. Take it or leave it!" I watched his face for signs that told me he knew he had met his match.

"No! This car is junk and I'm hauling it off!"

"You're just doing this to get even!" I said, really angry now.

"Even for what?" he asked.

I thought for a minute. "How about when you sneaked to the lake and I told Mom?"

"That was two years ago!" he said, his dander beginning to rise now.

"You've been waiting for the right time, and now you're getting even! Well, I'm going to ask Dad about it!" I said.

"Oooh, you mean a big-time, wheeling, dealing car buyer like yourself is telling Dad if she can't close the deal?"

"But I want that car and you don't, so why won't you sell it to me?"

"Because," he said, "if I sold you that scrapyard reject, I never would hear the end of it from Dad!"

"I wouldn't tell!" I said, not really thinking about where I could hide a car so it wouldn't be noticed.

"Look, if you want it that much, you can have it for nothing. At least it'll save me from having to haul it off," he said.

What kind of trick was this? What kind of pigeon did he take me for? Did he think I had just fallen off a hay wagon?

"I don't want it for free. This is my first car, and I want to pay for it myself."

Now I had really managed to set his teeth on edge.

"Give me a nickel," he said through clenched teeth.

"What for?" I asked.

"FOR THE CAR!" he yelled. "I'll sell it to you for a nickel!"

"SOLD!" I said with more enthusiasm than I had meant to show. Oh well, it didn't really matter. He definitely knew whom he was dealing with now!

"Where are the keys?" I asked, handing him a nickel.

"There aren't any. There are two wires under the dashboard. Lie down on the floorboard, and you'll see them. Touch those wires together and it'll start ... most of the time."

"But what if it doesn't?" I asked.

"Okay, try to park it facing downhill. These two bricks," he said, kicking two bricks from in front of the front tires, "are your emergency brakes. Kick them out from in front of the car and jump in as it rolls down the hill. Then just pop the clutch a couple of times, and most of the time it'll start."

"And what if it doesn't?" I asked, beginning to think I needed some change back from my nickel.

"Call a cab," he said, flipping the nickel in the air as he walked away. "Oh, by the way," he added, "if you ever decide to get rid of it, I'll haul it off for you—for fifteen bucks."

I began looking the car over and discovered a few things I hadn't noticed before.

For one thing, the front door on the driver's side wouldn't stay closed—it was tied together with an old electrical cord. When the motor started—which wasn't all that often—the windshield wipers came on. The only way to turn them off was to turn off the motor.

I had the windshield wipers taken off because people stared at me when I drove down the street on a sunny day with the wiper blades going ninety to nothing. But after the wipers were taken off, there were two little knobs left on the front of the windshield, that turned back and forth, making loud, irritating squeaks.

There was no window on the driver's side. When I went anyplace, my hair would be sticking straight up by the time I got there. But then again, that didn't happen all that often because you're not really going fast enough to get wind-blown when you're being towed behind another car—which *did* happen a lot.

All in all, I kept that car for about a month, and I figure I got my nickel's worth. Besides, when you get towed and pushed as much as I did, you rack up some unbelievable gas mileage.

I couldn't have gotten that kind of mileage if I had been driving a horse and buggy!

Oops!

Len and I have been married twenty-six years, and during that time I've learned a lot of do's and don'ts—not to mention a long list of things that come under the heading of "it doesn't really matter, anyhow."

One very useful thing I've learned is how to get the most mileage out of liver and onions. This works every time, but only because Len has also learned a few do's and don'ts.

It works like this: I fix liver and onions with mashed potatoes, peas, and salad on Monday. Then on Tuesday, I recycle the leftovers and we have liver and onions with potato patties (fixed with leftover mashed potatoes) and pea salad (fixed with leftover you-know-what).

Now, I love liver and onions, and having it two days running sounds good to me—but not as good as an enchilada dinner.

Len eats liver and onions because . . . it's there. And the only thing he likes less than liver and onions is leftover liver and onions. So every time we have that particular menu on one day, he calls from work the next day, checking on the fare for that night. I tell him, and he always pauses long enough to think he has made me think he's making a spur-of-the-moment decision. Then he casually suggests I meet him in town, and we'll go out for Mexican food.

Now that's what I call getting a lot of mileage out of one liver-and-onions meal.

Besides, being able to always count on certain things adds stability to the marriage. He can always count on leftovers the day after liver and onions, and I can always count on an enchilada dinner the day after liver and onions.

The other night we were having a "leftovers" day at the Mexican restaurant, and I was watching the waiter try to keep everyone happy. It was during the peak dinner hour, and they were obviously shorthanded that night.

He didn't have a problem with us because we were quite happy to be waiting on enchiladas instead of having instant liver and onions, but there were people there who didn't have liver and onions hanging over their heads, and they were beginning to get bent out of shape. (The mob was hungry and things could get nasty—there was talk of a lynching.)

Just when I thought he had things pretty well under control, he leaned over too far with a tray of three large iced teas—the kind you could swim in if you wanted to. They slid off and totally soaked the three ladies sitting there.

He apologized profusely, and the ladies were given their meal on the house. But later I saw them talking to him, and he took money out of his pocket three different times and gave it to the ladies. They were all wearing jeans and T-shirts. I couldn't see anything involving a cleaning bill, but they realized they had consumer power, and they used it.

I think all irate customers should first look at the situation from the other side of the counter before they blow their tops. It's a "walk a mile in my corn pads" deal.

I've been on the other side of that counter many times in my earlier years, and believe me, I have a world of respect for those people. They do hard work.

And think about this: Someone who waits tables several hours a day, day after day, is bound to have an accident every now and then. If we spent that much time in our own kitchen, we'd have more accidents than we already do.

Thinking back over the years when I was waitressing, I can recall some monumental mishaps, as I had my share. But there is one I had that was by far the most painful.

I was working for my dad in his café. He had two of those great big coffee urns, each one holding several gallons of coffee. In the afternoons, people from stores in the area would come into the café for their coffee break. I would have one urn already fixed with fresh coffee, and while the counter was filled with happy customers with full coffee cups, I would fix the other urn full of fresh coffee. In order to do that, I had to run the old, hot coffee out into a dishpan, and I'd stand on one of those wooden pop boxes and clean the machine out with a long-handled scrubber.

That day, the counter was full, as usual, but there was one difference: The boy who worked behind the soda fountain at the drugstore on the corner was there. I thought he looked so cute in his white apron and cap—I guess it was a matter of falling for a man in uniform.

Anyhow, I had my mind on other things besides that coffee urn. I had run the coffee into the dishpan and set it on the floor behind me, while I stood on the pop box cleaning the machine.

I had my back to the customers and was working with all of the diligence of a modern-day Cinderella.

While I worked, I wondered if the boy from the drugstore was watching me. And if he was, did he think I was as cute in my uniform as I thought he was in his. And would he eventually ask me out. Maybe we would get engaged and later married. We would live in a little vine-covered cottage, where I would wash and iron his uniforms and cook liver and onions for him.

I was so caught up in my fantasies that I forgot I had set the dishpan full of hot coffee on the floor behind me.

I held onto the edge of the cabinet and stepped down with my back still to the customers, hoping he was watching and taking note of the charming, unaffected way I moved as I stepped gracefully down—into that dishpan full of hot coffee!

That coffee was scalding hot and ankle deep! I have been known to linger over my coffee, but not that day!

The amazing thing is that I still had the thought in my mind of trying to impress that boy. I was absolutely blistered on that one foot, but I didn't want anyone to know it hurt, especially him! Maybe if I was calm enough, nobody at the counter would notice what I had done. Maybe they were all laughing at something else—sure they were!

I didn't stop to chat with anyone. I hurried to the back, and after I got behind the partition that separated the customer area from the kitchen, I let out a yell that could be heard in Philadelphia!

Eventually, I did go out with that boy, but he was cheese soufflé, while I was liver and onions, and never the twain shall meet.

Shhh!

My husband and I enjoy fishing about as much as it is possible to enjoy anything. The anticipation of waiting to see what you're going to catch is a lot of fun, but even if the fish aren't biting, just leaning back and relaxing is wonderful! In fact, there have been times when I was so comfortable and relaxed that I honestly hoped I wouldn't get a bite.

Fishing hasn't always been that relaxing. When our kids were little, we had a great time taking them fishing, but it wasn't exactly what you'd call relaxing. Of course, we were used to being around our kids, and we didn't really notice the hullabaloo that goes on when small kids are at the lake. I'm sure other people, who didn't have kids along, noticed.

I remember one couple in particular. Our son, Jim, was about twenty months old when we took him and our dog, Misty, to the lake.

These people were in a boat anchored a few yards from the shore where we were fishing. Now, I would like to say right here that since our kids have grown up, I have become acutely aware of the hullabaloo associated with some instances involving kids at the lake—and I said *some* instances. I enjoy watching kids have a good time at the lake, but there are some times when . . .

And for the couple in the boat that day, we were one of the "hullabaloo" instances they weren't enjoying. And to tell the truth, if we had changed places with that couple, we wouldn't have enjoyed us either.

As it was, we were having a great time! Jim was toddling around, squealing and laughing and running after Misty. And as for Misty, she was half Labrador and loved swimming as much as we loved fishing. Every now and then she'd jump into the lake, making quite a splash, which would cause Jim to laugh and squeal even louder.

We built a fire and made a pot of "creek-bank coffee." Since some of you aren't familiar with creek-bank coffee, I'll tell you how it's made. You fill the coffee pot with water and pour in the grounds— no filter, just coffee grounds and water. After it comes to a boil, you let the grounds settle a little in the bottom of the pot and—you have creek-bank coffee. At home, this coffee would be totally unacceptable, but at the lake it's pure gourmet!

Len and I each had a fishing line in the water and a cup of that grrrreat coffee, and we were basking in the glow of parenthood as we watched our young son romp with his puppy dog. Walt Disney himself could have written that scene!

But the couple in the boat weren't basking—they were more like simmering. I'm sure that every squeal and every splash went right through them, setting their teeth on edge.

I guess, too, it was made worse by the fact that they were anchored there before we came. They were sitting in their nice, quiet boat, listening to the gentle lapping of the waves, at peace with the world and—Boom!—we exploded on the scene.

The final insult added to injury came when Jim managed to make a bigger splash than Misty had.

He was standing by me, discussing world affairs from the viewpoint of a twenty-month old, when Misty charged down the hill off to one side of me and made a flying leap into the lake.

Jim thought that was really funny and before I knew what he was doing, he jumped in after her!

Len and I both yelled at the same time and grabbed him out of the water. When we got him back on the bank, he was choking and crying at the top of his lungs. Misty had climbed back out of the water and was barking because Jim was crying. Len and I were both trying to comfort Jim and hush Misty.

If that lake had been a road, that couple would have thrown gravel for a half mile when they dug out of there. As it was, they gunned that boat and took off, leaving a wall of waves washing into the bank. I was surprised they remembered to hoist their anchor and mizzen their mast and all that stuff.

Did we accept the blame for spoiling their fishing? Of course not. Actually, we didn't think of it at the time. If we had, we'd have probably just felt sorry for them because they weren't having as good a time as we were.

I suppose our kids have put a damper on their share of other people's fishing trips, but there was one couple that my husband can take credit for causing to pull up anchor and head for calmer waters.

This time, we were in a boat, too. Jim was around twelve years old and Chris was seven.

The boat was really small and had a motor just about equivalent to that of a push mower. So by the time we all got in with our fishing equipment, it sat very low in the water, and the motor really had its work cut out for it.

The boat trailer had lost one of the rollers that holds the boat up from the trailer and allows it to slide off into the water when it's being launched. We had to drive thirty-five miles into "the city" to pick up a part for it, so, until we did that, Len had put an old tennis shoe in place of the roller to keep the boat from hanging up on the trailer.

There were two launching ramps where we were, but there were several boats—really nice bass boats—waiting their turn to launch. We pulled our little dinghy in, wearing its old tennis shoe, and waited in line behind the "big boys" for our turn to take the plunge—and we hoped not literally.

As each boat was launched, it would roar off with such force that the front end of the boat would be sticking out of the water.

Our turn came, and while other boats waited for us to get through with the ramp, we discovered that although the tennis shoe probably helped some, it wasn't enough. Len and the kids and I tugged and pulled and pushed until we finally inched the boat off the trailer and into the water.

People waiting to use the ramp couldn't believe the whole situation. The kids couldn't either. As we went putt-putt-putting away from the dock with the front end sticking up out of the water, not from the power of the motor, but because there was too much weight in the back, the kids tried to lie down so people wouldn't see them.

By now, Len was not in the best of moods. He would rather have been driving one of those bass boats, but he refused to "give up the ship" and admit our boat was a little less than seaworthy.

The kids were wanting to go home before we ever got the boat off its tennis shoe. That thought was floating around in my mind, too, but I thought it best if I didn't verbalize it. I'd just make the best of it. Maybe if I could make the kids have a good time—How do you make kids have a good time? I couldn't really threaten them with being grounded if they didn't have a good time.

As we raced across the lake—I wished—as we putted across the lake, I heard myself say, in a tone of voice so "perky" that even I looked around to see who had said it, "Let's all sing 'Row, Row, Row Your Boat.' I'll start it."

This was met with such an ugly outburst from the kids and such a stony stare from Len that for one brief moment,

I thought I was going to be thrown overboard like chum bait to attract the fish.

Okay, so maybe we didn't have to have a good time. It wasn't like there was some kind of "Good Time Rule."

We putted around to several fishing spots with no luck. We'd fish a few minutes, and then Len would decide to move to another place. Each time we moved, the kids were protesting louder because they wanted to go home—and so did the boat.

When we first started across the lake, it seemed the little boat was saying, "I think I can, I think I can . . . ." But as we went from spot to spot, I thought it began to sound like it was saying, in a very wheezy voice, "Get off my back; get off my back."

Finally, we came to a big concrete tower that had something to do with controlling the water at the dam. It was a known bass hang-out, and a couple were there already, with their bass boat tied up, lure fishing.

Now, Len and I have never really been interested in lure fishing. We generally use bait.

Len tied our boat to the other side of the tower, and we dropped our lines into the water. Jim got out his little portable radio and turned it on to less than "easy listening." Chris began complaining that she needed to visit the ladies' room, and I found myself nervously humming "Row, Row, Row Your Boat" while Len tried to get his line untangled from some brush at the bottom of the lake.

The couple in the other boat kept glancing our way, hoping that they would get a glimpse of our leaving. And we might have obliged, but they had the misfortune of catching a pretty good-sized bass.

Len decided he should switch to a lure.

"Jim, have you still got that lure in the tackle box?" he asked.

Jim dug around through the tackle for a minute or so and then held up a big, blue, wooden lure with peeling paint and a couple of bedraggled yellow feathers that hid a rusty hook. It was enough to cause any fish to go on a diet.

But did that deter my husband? No way! Fish, Beware!

Even if they weren't hungry, all he had to do was manage to clunk one on the head when he cast that thing out and then wait for it to float to the top.

The way the boat was tied, he had to cast the length of the boat and over our heads to land off to the side of the tower where the bass seemed to be waiting for lunch.

He cast—we all ducked—and BINGO—he hooked the rope that the boat was tied to.

The kids and I exploded in laughter. You've heard that expression, "laughter is the best medicine"? Well, it depends on who is dispensing it and who is getting it.

At that particular moment, laughter wasn't exactly what Len had in mind for what ailed him. A new boat would have suited him much better.

He began expressing himself rather loudly, which made it almost impossible for us to stop laughing.

When things had calmed down and we had just about laughed ourselves into being made to swim home by the "Capitan" of the boat, I noticed that the bass-catching couple had left for calmer waters. And I'm sure any fish in the immediate area left with them.

Local fish restaurants owe us a word of thanks, because I'm sure that while our kids were growing up we caused many frustrated, empty-handed fishermen to show up at their doorstep for a fish dinner.

I just love the first fourteen verses of the twenty-first chapter of John. To sit down on the bank of the lake and eat fish and bread that Jesus had cooked! What a fish dinner!

And I like the part in verse 11, where it says that Peter dragged the net ashore with 153 large fish that the Lord had caused to get into the net. Not just fish, but large fish. If you want to go fishing, I think the Lord is the One you want to go with.

"Come, follow me," Jesus said, "and I will make you fishers of men" (Matthew 4:19).

Do You Feel a Draft?

When our kids were small, taking a vacation was something that had to be thought out and planned very carefully. There are so many things that have to be taken into consideration when you vacation with young children. You've got to find a place that the whole family will enjoy, so that puts a lid on any thoughts aimed toward azalea festivals, mountain climbing, or visits to any relatives who think all kids should be made to wear signs saying CAUTION, THIS PRODUCT CAN BE HAZARDOUS TO YOUR HEALTH.

You also have to find a place that you can afford because, let's face it, kids are expensive even in everyday life, and much more so on vacations where there is quite a bit of eating out involved. We thought about convincing the kids that "vacation" is another name for a trip to the grocery store, but we figured it probably wouldn't take long for the kids to want us to buy our groceries at Disneyland like their friends did sometimes.

Once you decide where you're going, you have to map out the route so you know where every rest stop is and how far it is from there to the next gas station rest room and from there to the next souvenir shop rest room and all of the convenient clumps of bushes in between these places.

I used to think that the motion of the car made kids subconsciously think of a boat, which caused them to think of water, which caused them to need a rest stop. But that's not it, because I've noticed that car motion doesn't affect them that way in town where there is access to rest rooms. It's just on the open road when parents are most likely to hear those three little words, *I can't wait!*

So, keeping all of this in mind, when our kids were six and eleven, we mapped and planned and discussed, and then we mapped and planned and discussed some more. We narrowed it down into four categories—Impractical, Impossible, Out of the Question, and You've Got to Be Kidding.

Finally, when we had eliminated everything but the local flea market, Jim said something absolutely brilliant: "Dad, why can't we go to Branson? Mike went, and he had a good time."

Out of the mouths of babes! Why hadn't we thought of that? We could drive to Branson with probably no more than a couple hundred "pit stops." What more could we ask!

So we loaded the car with suitcases, snacks, travel games, comic books, Chris's blanket that she wouldn't sleep without, her baby doll that she wouldn't sleep without, Jim's pillow that he wouldn't sleep without. . . . Loading the car took longer than the actual vacation.

But, finally, with both kids scrunched into the only remaining empty spaces in the backseat, and Len clutching the steering wheel with white knuckles and a determined set to his jaw, I made one final trip through the house to "batten down the hatches," and then—one more final trip back into the house because Chris couldn't wait until the first rest stop, and then—BRANSON, BEWARE—the Breedloves were coming!

We got there in time to spend a couple of hours in the amusement park before it closed, which made us eligible to go back the next day, using the same tickets. We love a bargain!

So, the next morning, bright and early, we were back at the park. The kids had a ball! And so did Len and I. We rode rides, ate, saw shows, ate, went down into the cave, ate, saw the crafts, ate—and just when we couldn't believe that we had eaten the whole thing—we ate some more.

By about five o'clock that evening, Len and I were stuffed, windblown, sunburned, and our skin was all wrinkled from getting wet on the water rides all day long. The kids were still going strong.

There was some entertainment scheduled to start at 5:30, so we found a bench to sit on while we waited.

Now I don't know how it happened, I only know that when I bent down to sit on the bench there was an odd sensation of freedom and a sudden draft where there hadn't been a draft a few seconds before. I quietly and quickly checked, and there was definitely a reason I was feeling a draft!

My pants had split in the seam from the waistband in the front, all the way down and around to the waistband in the back. The only thing holding the two pieces of my pants together was that waistband.

We had ridden water rides all day long, and my pants had gotten wet and stayed that way. I guess the chlorine or whatever they put in there to keep the water looking nice weakened the cotton thread in my pants.

When the pants gave way to the pressures of the times, I heard the rip. And while it sounded to me like the earth had split, no one else even heard it, not even my family.

Len was munching down on a caramel apple while he watched people walking by. Chris was seeing how far she could hop on one foot—and not always *her* foot. Jim was trying unsuccessfully to convince his dad that he could go on rides while we watched the show.

As for me, I was just quietly sitting there, with what was left of my dignity being held together by a one-inch-wide strip of cloth. I was afraid to move. This was worse than one of those dreams you have where you find yourself having gone someplace in your underwear. Because at least you can tell yourself it's a dream, and that'll be the truth. I was telling myself that it was a dream, but it wasn't—it was a nightmare!

Besides, I don't think you can feel things in dreams, and I could definitely feel that cool bench.

"Len, my pants split," I finally managed to say.

He put the last bite of apple in his mouth, "Are you sure?" he asked.

"I'm sure," I said, and I cautiously showed him what had happened.

He drew in a sharp breath and that last bite of apple went down the wrong way.

He was coughing his head off, and I was faced with a dilemma. Should I stand up in front of the whole world so I could do the Heimlich maneuver on him, or should I try to flag down a passerby—or maybe I could do that Heimlich maneuver sitting down? Decisions, decisions.

Fortunately, while I was pondering the situation, the piece of apple got back on track and went on its way, and our focus went back to the original problem.

No doubt about it, it was time to go back to the motel.

The trick was to do it without sending several hundred people into shock.

I stood up, and my family quickly surrounded me as we began shuffling in a tight little group toward the front gate. As we shuffled through the park, I had my head down, avoiding eye contact with anyone who might realize what was happening. Len and Jim were laughing and Chris was loudly objecting to having to leave the park.

People were looking at us as if we were the closest-knit family they had ever seen. I guess we did look funny, but I could have assured those people that we'd have looked a lot funnier if we hadn't been a "close-knit" family.

We were a long way from the front gate, but not nearly as far as it seemed. It seemed farther to that gate than it is from Oklahoma to Missouri.

When we finally got to the parking lot, my own home never looked as good to me as that car did! And once the kids were in the swimming pool back at the motel, they didn't mind having left early. Besides, they got to spend most of the day there and part of the day before, and that's a lot longer than they ever got to spend at the grocery store.

When I put those pants on that morning, the last thing I was thinking was that they would—pardon the pun—let me down, but they certainly did do that!

Thank goodness, God does a much better job than that when He dresses us!

"I delight greatly in the Lord; my soul rejoices in my God. For He has clothed me with garments of salvation and arrayed me in a robe of righteousness" (Isaiah 61:10).

I'll Take Chocolate

I was sitting in the waiting area of the airport not too long ago, and I overheard part of an interesting conversation. I wasn't eavesdropping, but the people were sitting directly behind me, and the only way I could not have heard would have been to put my fingers in my ears, which would have looked a little silly, so . . .

Anyhow, one lady was telling the other one about a friend of theirs who had lost a lot of weight on some kind of diet. She went on to say how good the friend looked.

The other lady said, "Yes, he does look good, but he's so boring now. All he ever talks about is what he ate and what he's going to eat!"

I can understand that. When you're in the middle of a serious diet you get kind of obsessed with your menu choices. Although, I have been on some of the fad diets where you didn't have any choices. In fact, I've been on just about every fad diet in the book—not all of them, because new ones come out every day, but I've been on my share.

And I'll tell you what—anybody who has been on one fad diet has probably been on a bunch of them because we all know fad diets are for the birds! Chubby birds at that, because fad diets wouldn't work for them, either. Besides, birds probably know better than to do something like that to their bodies. Can you imagine birds deciding to eat noth-ing but a half dozen sesame seeds a day—or maybe one of the "all you can eat diets" that would let them eat all of the sunflower seeds they wanted as long as they only ate the hulls and threw the nut part away?

I've been on some diets that were just that ridiculous. I think the silliest one I ever tried was called the "candy bar" diet.

Now, just the name alone can get fad dieters excited, especially if they are chocoholics like me.

On that diet, I was supposed to eat nothing but candy bars. I got one for each meal and two more for snacks. That was a total of five candy bars a day. Can you imagine!

I was so excited about that diet that the day before I started it I ate a couple of candy bars just for practice.

The way the candy bar diet was supposed to work was that all that sugar was supposed to give you all kinds of energy, which would cause you to move around a lot and burn that sugar off and—*Voilà*—off would come the extra pounds!

Well, it didn't do that for me, but it did give me the worst kidney infection I'd ever had in my entire life! And it made me hate candy bars for . . . a couple of days.

And then there was the "No-Diet Diet." Have you ever noticed that all of these fad diets have names that appeal to people who have done things to cause them to have to resort to a diet in order to get down to their desired weight? People who didn't particularly care if they ever ate a candy bar wouldn't be attracted to a candy bar diet. And likewise the No-Diet Diet—only someone who needed to diet would be attracted to a name like that.

The No-Diet Diet involved playing tennis while I wore a ten-pound weight belt around my waist. It was supposed to burn calories. I only did that one time. Maybe it burned a calorie or two, but it also rearranged most of my major internal organs. And maybe it wasn't all that bad—it only hurt when I laughed, talked, or breathed. For about a week it felt as if I had sprained everything I had.

The bottom line is, fad diets are anything but successful. But as long as there are people like me who think public buildings should be required to have candy bars mounted in glass cases on the walls with signs saying, "In Case of Emergency, Break Glass," there will be fad diets to tempt the temptable.

Chocolate is an awful temptation for me. I know there are all kinds of sugar-free chocolate out there, and some of it is good, too, but somehow ...

I do like chocolate. In fact, I wrote a poem extolling the virtues of the chocolate bar. It's called "Ode To a Chocolate Bar" and it goes like this:

> *Oh, chocolate bar, oh, chocolate bar,*
> *Your name is on my lips.*
> *But, alas, I've found,*
> *You are also on my hips!*

Anytime I've been on a diet, fad or otherwise, chocolate has been my downfall.

And when I said I understood how people on a diet can become so totally involved in their menu, I meant it, because I've been there.

Years ago, right after I graduated from high school (okay, so it was years *and years* ago), I worked for my uncle in his restaurant.

He served the best homemade cream pies in the entire world and maybe even the entire galaxy! They were wonderful pies! He had coconut, cherry, pineapple, and the ever popular—CHOCOLATE!

Almost every day I would eat a piece of chocolate cream pie and drink a cup of coffee. It was something I really looked forward to, but I never really gave it much advance thought. Coffee break would come and I'd say, "I think I'll have a cup of coffee and a piece of chocolate pie." It was more of a spur-of-the-moment decision than a habit—or so I thought.

Then came the time when those pies began to be on other places besides my mind, and it was fad diet time!

I don't remember what diet I tackled that time, but that was when I discovered I had an "emotional tie" to chocolate cream pie.

It hit me when I had my coffee break that first afternoon.

I said, "I think I'll have a cup of coffee and a—"

Words failed me. I just stood there speechless while the terrible truth began to sink in—chocolate cream pie wasn't on my diet list!

My eye began to twitch, my lips began to quiver, my mouth was watering, and I began wheezing—could it be I was allergic to diets that didn't have chocolate pie on their "can have" list?

Wait a minute, get hold of yourself, Connie, you know better than that. This was simply a matter of self-control. I would tell myself that I didn't want any chocolate pie, and even if I did—which I didn't—I wasn't giving myself any. Besides, like I said, I didn't even want any.

I pulled myself together, got a cup of coffee, and I think I drank it. I got through that first day.

The second day was unbelievable! I never knew it was possible to want a piece of chocolate pie as much as I wanted one.

That's when I began talking about it. I discovered that there were several things you could say about chocolate pie, and I said them all. The other waitresses thought I had finally lost it.

I began watching customers who were eating chocolate pie. I'm sure this made some of them very uncomfortable, but I couldn't help myself.

Finally, the inevitable happened. After the customers finished eating their meal, before we gave them their bill, we were supposed to ask, "Would you care for a piece of pie?"

There was a man at the counter who had just finished eating a hamburger. With my ticket book in hand, I walked up to him and said, "I'll take chocolate."

I don't know who looked more surprised, him or me. I was so embarrassed I wanted to crawl under the counter. But instead, I did the only thing there was to do. I just stood there, laughing.

Needless to say, he didn't order any pie, and he probably told people to watch out for that nut who worked behind the counter.

I knew then that it was time to have a coffee break and—a piece of pie!

Now, I'd like to say right here that I didn't do that, I really would, but I can't say that, because I went right to the kitchen and had the biggest piece of chocolate pie I could find. And I'd like to say I felt so guilty that I didn't enjoy one bite of it, but I can't say that, either, because, while I did feel guilty, that piece of pie was one of the best I'd ever tasted.

It's Knot Right!

When I go to an arts-and-crafts show, I'm always amazed by the things people make. It's unbelievable what some people can do with a bleach bottle or an empty toilet paper (TP) roll.

When I was growing up, we saved Popsicle sticks, and when we had enough of them, we'd make a little knick-knack box or something with them. But today you don't have to save Popsicle sticks. You can buy whole bags of them in the craft department of any variety store—and they've never even been used!

Actually, I think that kind of takes away from the charm of it. When we made something with Popsicle sticks, the sticks always had a faint color left from whatever flavor you'd had that day. It not only made for a colorful some-thing-or-other, but as you glued those sticks together you could think about the Popsicles you had eaten and enjoy them all over again in your mind.

There was something else we made along the arts-and-crafts line. In fourth grade art class every now and then we'd all be asked to bring a bar of soap to school, and we had a soap-carving lesson.

I remember I made a doghouse with mine. In fact, every time we had soap-carving day, I made a doghouse. It wasn't that I had any special attraction to doghouses, but they were easy to carve and didn't have to have a chimney on them.

We got to keep our carved things, but the teacher took all of the shavings home. I figure she didn't have to buy bath soap until she retired.

We made a lot of things in school, but only a few of them are still on my memory list. I remember one that was my all-time favorite. It was a tin can lid that had a picture of the Campbell's soup kids glued to it. We did that in the first grade.

Arts and crafts have become a lot more sophisticated. Maybe that's why I content myself with just admiring other people's efforts and confining my own to gluing pictures on tin cans.

Some people look at an empty TP roll and they see dolls, banks, suncatchers, wind chimes—a thousand things! I look at an empty TP roll and see something I'm out of and will probably forget to buy when I go to the grocery store.

But a friend of mine convinced me that somewhere, buried deep inside of me, was an arts-and-crafts wizard who, like the genie in the lamp, was begging to be turned loose on the world to do wonderful things with TP rolls.

There was a craft supply store that was offering a free five-day macramé class in exchange for our buying all of our macramé supplies from them. Looking back on this incident, I think that friend of mine didn't see a potential arts-and-crafts wizard as much as she really didn't want to take the class by herself.

But, armed with faith, hope, and two hundred miles of macramé rope, I jumped into the arts-and-crafts scene with a vengeance. Ever since I had watched my grade school art teacher carry home baskets of soap shavings, I had felt I was missing something. Maybe this class would fill that terrible void—maybe I could even learn to macramé a doghouse!

The first half hour went fine. We chose our patterns and bought our supplies. There were no doghouse patterns available, so I chose a hanging plant holder.

The thing is, I was like an onion in a field of petunias. All of the ladies in that class, including my friend, were old hands at arts and crafts. All of their homes were decorated with things they had made—and pretty things at that. Hours of hard work and a lot of TLC had been put into those things. All of their doors always had those pretty, seasonal wreaths on them made out of time cards and feathers and grapevines. My door had a note on it to remind me to get TP at the store.

I tried not to ask dumb questions, but when you know nothing about what you're doing, it's hard to tell if you're asking a legitimate question or not.

Evidently, by the end of that first lesson, the teacher had decided that I didn't know what a legitimate question is. I think my presence in the class was beginning to irritate her, kind of like a fly at a watermelon feed.

But that was okay. She couldn't help it if she didn't have the foresight to know a potential craft genius when she saw one. Besides, the less confidence she had in my ability as a crafter, the bigger her delight would be when she saw what was fixing to rise up out of the ashes of all of those wasted years and discarded bleach bottles and TP rolls.

Riding home after that first day, my friend casually asked if I was going back the next day.

"Yes, I am! What made you ask something like that?" I asked, really surprised by her doubt.

"Nothing. It just doesn't seem like you're enjoying this very much," she said.

"Of course I'm enjoying it!" I answered, thinking to myself that I hadn't enjoyed anything that much since I fell off of a horse and broke my arm in three places.

The second day went about like the first one, and as my friend let me out of the car she said, "Are you going tomorrow?"

"Yes! Why do you keep asking me that?" I said, rather impatiently.

"I just wanted to know whether to come by for you," she answered.

Did she know something that I didn't? Oh, well, three more days.

But when the next day came, I was dreading it so much I decided that this would be my last lesson. I could learn more than enough in three days to satisfy my curiosity about macramé. Besides, I had a new bar of bath soap, and I hadn't made a doghouse in years.

I didn't tell anyone that I was quitting. I just figured I'd casually mention it at the end of the lesson.

That day there were nine of us sitting around a big table macraméing and visiting. We each had six, eight-foot-long strands of macramé cord that we were working with.

As the instructor came by each of us, she had us hold up our work for her to see.

My fingers were sore, but my work looked downright respectable. I couldn't wait to tell her I wasn't coming back. She was going to be sorry to lose a talent like mine.

When she got to me, I held my work up and braced myself for the gasps of awe as my handiwork came to light and these ladies realized they had been sitting next to greatness.

It didn't happen. There were some giggles from some of the ladies, but you don't giggle at greatness. And the look on the instructor's face wasn't what I had expected, either. She looked kind of tired and defeated.

Looking closer at the work I was holding up, I spotted the problem. I had somehow woven my macramé project into two strands of rope belonging to the lady sitting next to me.

So, maybe the instructor wouldn't be sorry to see me go.

I sure wasn't going to be sorry to see me go, either. I was glad the whole ordeal was almost over. And there certainly was no need to tell her I wouldn't be back. The look of sheer joy on her face would be too much for my injured pride. I just wouldn't show up the next day.

But what happened next put a new perspective on the situation. I unraveled the extra rope I had "borrowed," and as we all gathered our things to go home, the instructor asked me if I was coming back the next day! I couldn't believe she would ask me something like that in front of everybody! And from the looks on the faces of some of the other ladies, I could see they couldn't believe it, either. It was a very embarrassing, awkward moment for me.

I really hadn't expected her to say something like that, but as unexpected as her question was, my answer surprised me even more!

"Of course I'm coming back! I wouldn't miss it for the world!" I heard myself say, and I smiled when I said it.

But I wasn't smiling on the inside. On the inside I couldn't believe what I had just said! Had I completely lost my mind? I didn't *want* to come back the next day! But human nature being what it is, I'd be back. It was just the principle of the whole thing—to think I'd let her intimidate me into staying home.

So, I came back the next day and the next day. I finished the entire week. On that last day, as I walked out the door, I felt as though I had run a hard race and won.

But if you get right down to it, I don't know if I won or not. I told myself there was no way she was going to run me off, so I let her attitude cause me to stay someplace I didn't want to be and do something I didn't enjoy doing. It was a catch-22.

But I still enjoy going to arts-and-crafts shows. And in a few days, I'm going to the biggest arts-and-crafts show of all! It's the drive down through the Arbuckle Mountains. The foliage is turning, and it's gorgeous down there right now.

When it comes to beautiful work, God is definitely the Master of arts and crafts!

"In the beginning God created the heavens and the earth" (Genesis 1:1).

I Didn't See That!

Years ago, I saw something—and that's *saw*, not *thought* I saw—my family is still kidding me about. They never did believe me. It wasn't a UFO or a giant gorilla sitting on top of our garage, swatting at airplanes. It was a very small—about ten inches long—alligator, walking across our driveway.

If you live in Florida, you're saying, "So what?"

But we were living in Dallas, and alligators were not considered native to Big D. We had a few armadillos that would wander in from time to time. And the people across the street had a pet boa constrictor that sunned itself in their yard, but no alligators—except one, and *I* saw it!

I was mowing the front yard when I happened to see it sitting in the middle of our driveway. It was sitting with its head raised up and its mouth about halfway open so that I could plainly see a small set of teeth.

I made a dash for the house to get my mom and dad so we could catch it. I ran in, yelling, "Come out here, quick! There's an alligator in the driveway!"

They could tell from my tone of voice, the look on my face, and my wild arm gestures that I had really seen an ALLIGATOR in the driveway!

When we got back out to the driveway—no 'gator.

"It's around here someplace," I said, looking in the flower bed.

"Connie, you saw a lizard," my dad said.

"I saw its teeth, and lizards don't have teeth!"

"Maybe the lizard had something in its mouth," my mother volunteered.

"Yeah," I said, "a full set of teeth, and it wasn't a lizard, it was an alligator!"

My dad started back into the house, "It's hot out here. Let's go back in and talk about it."

Talk about it? Were they humoring me? *They were humoring me!*

"What's to talk about? I saw an alligator! There's an alligator out here!"

The man next door came over. "What are you all looking for? Morley's snake didn't decide to go visiting again, did it?"

"No, it's an alligator. I saw a little alligator in our driveway."

"It was probably one of those big lizards," he said knowingly. "There's a lot of them around here. Ugly ol' things, too. I know one time I—"

"It wasn't an ugly lizard. It was a kind-of-cute, little baby alligator with teeth!" I was beginning to get a little miffed. I knew what I had seen!

They never did believe me. The neighbor went back home muttering something to himself about the effects of TV on young people these days. My parents went back in the house agreeing with each other that I needed to do any future lawn mowing the cool of the evening, while wearing a hat to protect my head from the sun.

I never saw the alligator again. But once was enough. I saw what I saw!

The thing is, this happened in the late fifties, when it was still legal to sell baby alligators at Mardi Gras in New Orleans. A lot of people bought them.

I remember a couple of years later, some lady ran an ad in the paper in an effort to find her lost alligator—in Dallas, I might add. I know one thing, this happened about thirty-seven years ago, and I don't know where that alligator is now, but I bet he's past the "cute" stage.

Sometimes there is wisdom in seeing something but not saying anything, as I learned later. The situation involved not an alligator, but a pair of socks.

I was working at a large electronics plant in Dallas. I worked alone in a room that had a glass wall that allowed people in the hall to observe. Most of the time, that hall was pretty empty unless it was break time.

My job was to take strings of capacitors out of big tanks filled with acid and water, rinse them, and then put them in a drying oven. Just getting ready to take units out of the tanks and put them into the ovens was a job in itself. I had to wear a white lab coat (which looked very scientific), cloth gloves, rubber gloves over those, and finally a huge pair of heat-proof gloves over the other two pair.

On this particular day, it was raining cats and dogs when I went to work. I got my feet soaked just getting in from the parking lot. I was wearing bobby socks, and after they got so wet, the tops stretched out and looked really terrible.

The racks I dried units on were just metal frames, kind of like boxes without sides; and they had hooks up and down both sides to hang unit bars on.

The hall was deserted, no one around to see what I was doing, so I took off my socks and hung them on a rack in the oven.

I went on about my business.

I was so absorbed in what I was doing that I didn't notice a group of people gathered outside the window, watching me work. It was a group of businessmen from Japan, who were taking a tour of the plant.

I had to take some units out of the tanks and put them into the ovens, so I put on all of my gloves, right there in front of the window. I still didn't notice I was being watched.

I opened the oven and took out the rack that had my socks on it. As I turned toward the window, I found myself literally face-to-face with that group of businessmen. I remember one, in particular, had his hands behind his back and was craning his head forward to get a closer look at what I had on that rack.

For one terrible minute, I just froze while they all stared at me and my socks, and I stared back at them. Then I did the only thing I could do: I set the rack down to cool with the other racks and went on working like nothing was out of the norm.

I fully expected my foreman to come bursting in the door and escort me down to personnel. But he didn't. And not only that, nothing at all was ever said about it. I couldn't believe it! If he'd gotten any word at all, I'd have known it. The only thing I could figure was, no one in that group wanted to admit to anyone else that they thought they saw socks drying on that rack. So they all just finished the tour, said nothing, and went home. They probably weighed the chances of those really being socks and decided it was best to say nothing. I know it was best for me.

Whatcha Mean, Get Organized?

I've always admired people who are organized. I'm just sort of in awe of them. How do they get that way? Is it a genetic thing like having naturally curly hair? Or is it something you can learn like good manners? If it can be learned, then I don't know what the problem is because I've tried for years with little or no success.

I've learned to do other things. I can ride a bicycle. I can make gravy—and that one wasn't easy. Actually, the trick to that is to get your family used to having their gravy in slices. It gets a little awkward in restaurants when your kids order biscuits and a slice of gravy, and then you have to try to explain to them what that runny stuff on their plate is. You tell them very quietly to just eat it and not make a fuss because not everybody can make gravy like they get at home.

But being organized is something that has escaped me. I still try—I don't think I should just give up and slowly sink beneath the waves of unfolded clothes, forgotten appointments, and missed flights.

So, I continue to work at it. However, I think being organized can be carried too far. That sounds like sour grapes, doesn't it?—If I can't be organized, then who needs it!!! No, no, no—I don't feel that way. In fact, I'd give my eyeteeth to get organized. And I'm sure my husband would think he was in the wrong house if everything always went as smoothly as I would like.

A few years ago, there was an elderly, retired couple who lived down the street from us. Their family was grown, they didn't have to worry about going to work—they absolutely had it made! Can you imagine the fishing they could have done? But they diverted most of their energy and time to their yard.

That yard became the focus of their life. I wouldn't have been surprised to see plant food and fertilizer gift-wrapped and under their Christmas tree every year. The tags on the packages would naturally have the yard's name on them—"Our Yard."

"Our Yard" (their yard) definitely was gorgeous, no doubt about it. Every blade of grass in that yard was exactly the same length as every other blade of grass.

Butterflies had to make an appointment before they could land on the flowers. Birds weren't allowed in the yard at all unless they cleaned up after themselves. We'd see all of these birds out there with tiny, little brooms and pooper scoopers, making sure there was no trace of their having visited.

But all of the work and time spent showed. The entire neighborhood enjoyed looking at a beautiful yard like that. People would drive by just to look at "Our Yard" (their yard), and they would say things like, "Look at the work those people have done on that yard!"

They would drive by our yard (our yard), and they'd say, "I'll bet those people fish often."

I have to admit right here and now that I not only admired that couple's diligence, but deep down I envied the organized way they worked. They knew just exactly when to prune, mulch, and fertilize. I have seen that man mowing his grass in the rain because it was grass-mowing day.

But the topper came one day in the late fall. They had a little, half-grown tree, about six or seven feet tall, and most of the leaves had already fallen off and been promptly raked up.

I decided maybe it was time to do a little raking myself, so with rake and yard bags in hand, I prepared to attack the ankle-deep leaves that were carpeting the front yard.

As I worked, I was enveloped in an almost pious feeling of good citizenship, and I wondered if the organized couple was taking note of my labors. I casually looked in the direction of their house. I stopped raking and just stood there trying to grasp what I was seeing.

They each had a bag and a little step chair and were picking the remaining leaves off the tree before they could fall to the ground.

Now, that scared me. That was organization running amok!

I dropped my rake, ran into the house, grabbed my fishing pole, and left for safer ground.

But since then, I've developed my own organized method of taking care of the leaf situation, and it really works!

To begin with, don't rake the leaves at all. After they have all fallen to the ground, wait for a good wind to blow them into the neighbor's yard. Then, when you see your neighbors out raking leaves, take them a cup of hot chocolate to warm them up, and visit with them while they rake the leaves. When they are finished, your yard looks nice, their yard looks nice, and they have good feelings toward you because you took them hot chocolate. Now *that's* organization. There may be hope for me yet!

Actually, I do love the fall, when the leaves change color. God is such an artist. Every year, I'm totally amazed all over again when I see the colors He uses.

In Revelation there's a verse that talks about the tree of life, which stands on each side of the river that flows from God's throne. "And the leaves of the tree are for the healing of the nations" (Revelation 22:2).

Those leaves don't have to be raked.

And Baby Makes Three

When I was expecting my first child, I did everything in my power to get ready for that new experience of motherhood. I exercised, I ate healthy food, and I took prenatal vitamins.

I read every child-rearing book I could get my hands on. I had stacks of little gowns and diapers, mountains of baby powder, and oceans of baby oil.

I stockpiled enough baby food to keep my child stuffed until he graduated from college.

I have never been so totally prepared for anything in my whole life. I have never been so totally confident in my whole life as I was during that nine months. Nor have I ever, in my whole life, seen so much preparation and confidence fly out the window as fast as mine did.

To begin with, we lived a few miles out of town. But we knew exactly where the hospital was, so we weren't really concerned about getting there in time for the big event.

When my first contraction hit, it was so slight that I didn't really think about its being a labor pain. Besides, the baby wouldn't be coming that night because there was a TV special coming on that I had been waiting for some time to see ...

The second labor pain made me stop and try to think what I might have eaten that afternoon that could be giving me such a stomach ache.

The third one hit, and I began to realize that this baby obviously had not read the TV schedule.

By this time, Len was two hours late getting home from work. Since we were expecting a new family member, Len had always been glad to put in overtime, but tonight was not the night to work late. Regardless of overtime pay, TV programs, or anything else, this baby was making his debut into society!

Since Len was driving our only vehicle, I called the place where he worked to tell him I needed a ride to the hospital. The person who answered the phone said Len wasn't working late that night. Well, I figured, he must have stopped at the store for another stuffed animal. He had been stockpiling them.

And anyway, I had three alternative numbers to call—my parents, my brother, and my sister. I called them to let everyone know what was going on—none of them were home.

Now, I realized that at that particular moment, all of my preparation counted for exactly nothing—zero—zilch!

Okay, so now what? Well, in the movies they always boiled water. I guess I could do that—Wait a minute. Someone else was supposed to boil the water, not the person having the baby.

I called everyone's house again. No answer. Where was everybody? Didn't they know I was expecting a baby? Did they think that all of this weight I'd been gaining the last nine months was all potatoes and gravy?

Well, maybe I would boil some water, and if nothing else, have a cup of tea. Maybe that would calm my nerves and the labor pains would go away. Yeah, right!

Another pain hit. I called everyone's house again, only this time I dialed a whole lot faster. No answer.

Okay, that's it! No more Mrs. Nice Person. If they don't want to cooperate, then I'm going to just forget the whole thing!

I'll just have this cup of tea, watch my TV special, and go to bed early!

OUCH! That was a really good one, and much closer than the one before. Okay, I'll give them one more chance— I called everyone again, still no answer.

The people across the road weren't home, but their son's bicycle was out in the yard. Maybe ... I got a picture in my mind of me pedaling the six miles into town to the hospital, staunchly biting my lip to keep from crying out in pain, and stopping only once to help a little old lady change a flat tire.

Well, maybe that was a bit much, but I did know I had to do something. I guess I needed to think about calling some sort of emergency help. So, should I call the police department, the ambulance, or the fire department? I had heard of instances where all of these people had, at one time or another, delivered babies on the way to the hospital.

Maybe I should call all three and just go with the first one that got there.

I was debating the situation when I heard Len's pick-up truck in the driveway. The only thing that could have possibly sounded as good to me then would have been Gabriel's horn!

I hurried to the door as fast as my condition allowed.

There was Len's truck with a whole convoy of my family's cars behind him. I was so glad to see everyone that I didn't even wonder why the whole group had come to my house.

They all got out of their cars, but instead of coming to me on the porch, they stopped at Len's pick-up.

"Honey, look what your folks got us," he said, patting the arm of a couch in the back of his truck.

"My labor pains have started," I replied.

"I knew yesterday that they had bought it, but we wanted to surprise you," he said, not listening to what I had said.

"My labor pains started an hour ago," I said again, this time with a little more urgency.

"Come here and look and this," my mother said, also not listening to what I had said.

"I'M HAVING MY BABY!" I yelled, beginning to feel like I was dreaming that I was running in slow motion to the hospital, while my family stood around visiting with each other.

"Yes, and when the baby gets here, your living room will look nice, and there will be plenty of room for people to sit," my sister-in-law said.

Well, maybe a bicycle ride wouldn't be that bad after all.

I gave it one more try. "I'M HAVING MY BABY NOW! RIGHT NOW—AND IF SOMEBODY DOESN'T GIVE ME A RIDE TO THE HOSPITAL, I'M GOING TO HAVE IT RIGHT HERE IN THE FRONT YARD!" I yelled.

There was a moment of total silence while my words finally sank in on my family. I was almost thrown into the truck and Len peeled out, heading for the hospital.

Well, I didn't have my baby in the front yard. In fact, my son decided to wait five more hours before he put in an appearance. I think he just wanted to make sure he had everyone's attention before he made his grand entrance to the world.

But after I took him home, I discovered that although the advance preparation made things much easier, it still didn't equip me for some of the mishaps of motherhood.

There was one in particular that I remember because it was so embarrassing.

Jim was about four weeks old, and I was still trying to learn how to take care of this new little being while I kept the household in some sort of order. And it wasn't really working the way the baby books promised that it would. But, in all fairness to the baby books, I wasn't really organized before the baby came.

I think it would be nice if having a baby released some sort of "organization hormones" into your body, but it just doesn't work that way.

I think if you're organized before you have a baby, then that organization is sort of fine-tuned, and you find yourself clicking along like you had done this all of your life. Maybe. And if you're not organized—well, you know the rest.

Anyhow, I had an appointment to get my hair cut. I bundled Jim up, put him in his carrier, and set the carrier in the living room chair, while I put on my coat.

In keeping with my unorganized methods, I set his carrier on a small pile of unfolded clothes I had taken out of the dryer with the intent of folding them when I got back from the beauty shop.

When I picked Jim up, without realizing it, I also picked up a pair of Len's underwear. The baby blanket was bulky, and I had the underwear caught up in the blanket and didn't realize it.

I put Jim, the carrier, and the underwear in the car and went to the beauty shop. When I got there, I picked up Jim, the carrier, and the underwear again.

When I went into the shop, it was pretty busy, and I had to wait a few minutes. So I walked over to the lady who did my hair and showed her and two or three other ladies my pride and joy.

They were "ooohing" and "aahhing," and I was beaming with pride when I felt something fall on my foot. I had to crane my neck around Jim's carrier to see what had fallen out. When I did, the ladies all automatically looked down to see what I was looking at.

There was Len's underwear in all its splendor, lying on the floor of the beauty shop.

One of the ladies let out a squeal, and they all started laughing so loudly I was sure it would attract the attention of people for blocks around. It didn't, but it sure attracted everyone's attention in that shop.

That night, I told Len what a star attraction his under-wear had been in the beauty shop that day—he was not impressed.

But, looking on the bright side, it was one of his good pair. You know, the kind your mother always told you to wear in case you have to go to the emergency room. Or the beauty shop.

Both of our kids are grown now, and they both managed to survive having an unorganized mom. I had it all together for the really important things like school parties, zoo trips, cookie baking, and things like that. And we all had a good time.

As for organizing my life, I'm still working on that.

And I have a feeling that's something I'll always have to work on. But that's okay. It gives me something to do now that the really important things are finished, like zoo trips, school parties, baking cookies and good stuff like that. . . .

Car Wars

A couple of months ago we traded our car in, and I felt as if I were saying good-bye to an old friend. I drove by that lot yesterday, and the car was still sitting there, I felt like a traitor! I ducked down, hoping to avoid headlight contact with her. I didn't want her to see me with another car.

But I think she caught sight of me, and I'm almost positive I saw a tear glistening on her windshield.

I was glad to see they had fixed her grille. She'd been needing dental work for quite some time.

I thought about disguising myself with a wig and sunglasses and going by just to see how she was doing, but I was afraid she'd recognize my voice. Besides, I don't think I could take it if anyone came by and kicked her tires while I was there.

I think it's best if I don't go back there again—she might try to follow me home.

Now, that's the way I feel about it. If the car could *really* talk, the conversation would be more like this: "Oh, no, there's my old owner. Quick, somebody hide me, please! This is the first time in years that I've been really clean—no Coke spills on my floorboard, no dog hair all over my seats—and not even *one* cat's pawprint anywhere on my hood! Help! Keep her away from me!"

Every now and then you hear someone wish we still used horses and buggies instead of cars. I get that way myself sometimes when the car gets in one of its "moods," and decides to "sit this one out." I bet our cars would think twice about being moody if we treated them like a regular horse. Can you imagine that instead of taking your car to a mechanic to fix some problem, you just pull out a gun and shoot it? There have been a few times when that was a temptation.

If I didn't know better, I'd think cars have an intelligent mind—and they probably say the same thing about us. It seems they choose the most inopportune times to run out of gas or have a flat or—just take the day off!

I remember one car especially that I had before I got married. That car couldn't tolerate heat. I was living in Dallas then, and it gets pretty warm there in the summertime. Every time we went anyplace, that car would be huffing and puffing and hotter than a firecracker. I'd have to let it cool down before I could drive it again.

One afternoon, I took my youngest sister, Ginny, who was five at the time, to the lake to go swimming. The lake was only seven or eight miles from the house, so it shouldn't have been a problem for my car. But that car was a lot like some people—*everything* was a problem for it.

By the time we got there, the car was registering its usual complaints, and the radiator was doing its rendition of "I've Got Ssssssssteam Heat!"

The parking area was up on a hill with the lake down below it. I parked the car and raised the hood, then, with Ginny in tow, I headed for the cool water in the lake.

And so did the car. Only it waited until we got in the water and had our backs to the bank.

It was a regular swimming area, and there were several people swimming. I heard people yelling, but I didn't know what the ruckus was about until I heard the car hit the water.

I knew then what had happened before I ever turned around to look.

I don't know if I left it out of gear or if it slipped out of gear—I'm suspicious that when it saw us splashing around in that lake, it just felt the urge to go for a swim.

By the time that car got to the bottom of the hill it had gained so much momentum that I doubt its wheels were even touching the ground. It hit that water and kept on truckin'.

Looking back on that incident, I think I must have been a little bit in shock. I was so calm, you'd think my car was sitting at a car wash instead of in the lake. When I got to the car, I could see that the motor was completely under water. But all I could think of was to get in the car and drive it out.

The door wouldn't open because of the pressure of the water. So I put my foot against the back door and pulled on the front door with every ounce of strength I could muster. The door opened just a little crack, which was enough for the lake to surge in and not only open the door, but bend it all the way back against the front of the car.

When the car went into the lake, the windows were up, so at that point not much water was inside the car. Until, of course, compliments of me and the lake, the door was torn open and that car filled up like a water jug.

The water rushed in with such force it caused the glove compartment to fly open, and everything inside of it, including my dad's little book of road maps that I had borrowed and not returned, was floating around in the front seat.

Now I'm standing there, looking at the total ruination of my car, and my little sister said, in a very "uh oh, now you're in trouble" tone of voice, "Uhhhhm. Daddy's book is wet. He's going to be mad!"

There was a man there mowing around the lake with a tractor, and he hooked a chain on the back of my car and pulled it out of the lake for me. But we couldn't get the door to close before he pulled me out, so the force of the water as the car came out of the lake tore the door partially off.

One thing is certain: That's the fastest that car ever cooled off!

But the best part is that no one was hit by that thing. I appreciated the Lord for that, and I imagine some of those other swimmers did, too.

I wonder sometimes if Henry Ford realized what he was releasing on the world when he popularized the automobile. The economy is so dependent on motorization, though.

On the other hand, people are so inventive, if the automobile industry hadn't come along, we'd have made up for it in other ways. Horses would have continued to grow as a major industry. And someone would still have invented the quickie grocery stores, only the names would be different. There'd be names like Cash 'n' Carriage, Hurry 'n' Surrey, Stop 'n' Gallop, Nag 'n' Bag—maybe even a fast-food place called Wolf It 'n' Hoof It. There are all kinds of possibilities.

Actually, when you get right down to it, it doesn't really matter what mode of transportation we use right now. The main thing is that whatever we use now, that's not what we're going to have to use to get to heaven, thank goodness!

"The Lord will rescue me from every evil attack and will bring me safely to his heavenly kingdom. To him be glory for ever and ever. Amen" (2 Timothy 4:18).

Whoa!

My husband has a tractor that he talks to and babies as if it were a real person. It's one of those with two huge wheels on the sides, and two little ones on the front. It reminds me of those dinosaurs we used to see in the old Saturday afternoon matinees. The ones with two great big hind legs and two little tiny front ones. The little front legs made them look kind of vulnerable, and I always felt sorry for them when the hero of the movie won the fights.

One of the tires went flat once, and the tractor had to sit in the yard for a few days before Len could take off the tire and take it to town to be fixed. That tractor looked so forlorn and lopsided sitting there like that, I felt as sorry for it as I used to for those dinosaurs in the movies.

And I must say, it was very charitable of me to have compassion for that thing. It sure doesn't like me! I know machinery isn't supposed to be able to express feelings, but I don't believe that for a minute!

And I'll tell you something else: The other day when I was walking by it, I think I heard it growl at me.

But it needn't worry. I'm not going to mess with it. That tractor and I came to an understanding a long time ago: It'll leave me alone if I leave it alone.

There was a time when we didn't have an agreement like that. Right after Len bought it, he decided to teach me how to drive the thing.

Now, I wasn't too comfortable with that idea. I try to avoid anything that gives the appearance of crouching.

Len convinced me that all respectable farm wives know how to drive a tractor. But I had never seen a tractor at the grocery store or picking up kids after school, but then what did I know? He was the one raised on a farm, not me. I was a city girl.

I told him that maybe I should get a tractor license first, but he said I didn't need one. I had never heard anything so illogical in my life! I have to have a license to go fishing, for crying out loud, but it was okay for me to hop up on two tons of metal and take off? Where was the sanity in that?

Oh, well, country living has a lot of weird ways. Personally, I never could see the point of milking cows and gathering eggs when you could find that stuff already packaged and ready to go at the grocery store.

I put the tractor lesson off for as long as I could, but the day finally arrived when nothing I said would convince him to let me content myself with operating nothing more aggressive than a riding lawn mower.

I walked slowly to the barn—this wasn't my cup of tea.

How would he like it if I insisted that he learn how to run the washing machine? Actually, he knew how to do that. It was separating the clothes he seemed to have a problem with.

"Okay. I'm ready," I said, eyeing the tractor with a certain amount of distrust.

"Climb aboard!" he said cheerfully.

"Alone?" I couldn't believe he wanted me to drive solo right off the bat.

"There's not room for both of us up there. Don't worry, you're gonna love it!" he replied.

As I climbed up, it seemed the tractor gave a little shudder. I looked at Len to see what the deal was, but he didn't seem to notice anything.

"Now, push the clutch in."

"Where is it?"

"It's right there, the same place as on a car. Just think of this as a car."

How could I think of it as a car? I already thought of it as a flesh-eating dinosaur.

"Okay, now turn the ignition on and put it in gear just like you'd do in a car."

There was that car stuff again. No way. There was nothing about this thing that could be remotely compared to a car. A car had soft seats and a radio and a glove compartment with the auto club number in it if I got in trouble.

Oh, and there was one more thing a car had that this green monster didn't have—power steering.

I really didn't think about the steering part. I pushed down the clutch, started the engine, and put the tractor in gear. It took off like a house on fire!

Len was cheering me on like I was driving the Indy 500. I went in a straight line down the hill going toward the house. When I didn't turn at the place I was supposed to, Len stopped cheering and started yelling.

"Turn the steering wheel!"

"I can't! It won't turn!"

He was running along beside the tractor, shouting instructions and waving his arms. The instructions I understood. The arm waving was a nervous reaction to the house coming closer with each bounce of that tractor. If I hadn't been afraid to let go of the steering wheel, I'd have been waving my arms, too.

"Turn the steering wheel! You're going to hit the house!!"

"I know that, but it won't turn!!

"TURN IT HARD!" he yelled.

I turned it as hard as I could, and it turned enough to clear the house, but the porch was still in the line of fire. By then we were really running out of time, and so was the front porch.

Now, the front porch was just a small metal one that was attached to the trailer house. It probably would have just torn loose from the trailer without doing that much damage, but one of our famous "cellar holes" was a few yards on the other side of the porch. That concerned me a lot!

"Turn off the ignition!" Len shouted.

Now why hadn't I thought of that? Because I was scared out of my mind, that's why!

I turned the ignition off and the tractor stopped about a foot from the trailer house.

I sat there waiting for my legs to decide if they were ready to hold me up or not before I climbed down from the beast.

"Okay, honey, put it in reverse just like you would a car . . ." Len was saying.

"Are you out of your mind?" I said, practically falling off the tractor before it decided to take Len up on his suggestion and take off on its own. "I'm not driving this thing again! I don't want to learn to drive a tractor! I'm not going to learn to drive a tractor! I wouldn't even ride in a sidecar on a tractor!"

"Okay, Okay! I believe you. But are you really sure you won't try one more time? You know what they say about falling off a horse."

"Yeah, I do. I fell off a horse and broke my arm! Thank you, but no thank you!" I closed the conversation by heading for the house, but as I did, I watched that tractor out of the corner of my eye to make sure it didn't follow me in.

Driving lessons weren't discussed after that, but that tractor was a burr under my saddle. Every time I went outside it seemed that mean machine was sitting there smirking.

There is nothing in the world more infuriating than a tractor with an attitude Finally, one weekend it all came to a head. I couldn't take it anymore.

It had rained on and off all day, and my whole family was in the middle of a very serious afternoon nap. I was standing in the doorway, looking out at the soggy weather when that tractor caught my eye.

Now I knew that the whole episode had been blown way out of proportion. I knew the tractor was just a tractor—maybe a smart aleck one, but . . .

I walked outside and stood looking at it. This mindless hunk of junk. This "Green Acres" reject.

"So, you think it's over? Not yet, buddy!" I said, using the "make-my-day voice" that I usually used only in traffic.

"Mom, are you talking to the tractor?"

I turned to see my ten-year-old son standing behind me, with a questioning look on his face.

"No, I was just talking to myself," I said, climbing up on the tractor.

"Are you going to drive that!?" he asked, looking at me as though I were about to board a rocket to the moon.

"I'm going to surprise Dad," I answered.

He turned and ran into the house. I knew he had gone to wake up Len, but that was okay, because Len is so hard to wake up that I could not only learn to drive this thing, I could get a couple of fields plowed before he got out there.

I sat there looking at the foot pedals and gear shift, going over in my mind what each thing did and where each thing belonged at what time.

I took a deep breath, pushed the clutch down, and turned on the ignition.

Then everything happened at once. This machine had fooled me into thinking it was just cold metal. This thing was out to get me!

It reared up on its hind legs like a horse. In fact, I thought I heard it whinny. As it reared up, I saw Len standing in the doorway waving his arms again. I was glad he could wave his arms. I sure couldn't let go long enough to wave mine.

My feet were wet when I climbed up on that tractor. Just as the motor kicked in, my foot slipped off the clutch, and I had "popped a wheelie." It scared me worse than the first time.

I was grateful for Len's explanation, because for one awful minute there I felt as if I were in one of those horror movies where the machinery chases people around.

Every now and then, Len tries to get me to learn how to drive his "baby," but one person's "baby" is another person's nightmare.

Besides, looking at it from a logical point of view, why do I need to learn to drive a tractor? I can't think of any good reason, unless it would be to show myself that I can do it. And that's not a good reason, because after talking to myself about it, I discovered that it doesn't matter to me whether or not I can drive one of those things.

And as far as trying to impress Len with my tractor driving abilities, that doesn't matter either, because he still hasn't learned to sort laundry!

Tall in the Saddle . . .
For a Few Minutes

Riding horses is not what I do best. In fact, I guess it may be rated as the thing I do worst.

But in all fairness, when I was growing up, we didn't have those little mechanical horses at the grocery store to practice on. Today, by the time kids are seven years old, they've racked up enough hours on those things to qualify as jockeys in the Kentucky Derby.

The closest thing we had to the mechanical horses was the merry-go-round at the fair. That only happened once a year, so it really wasn't enough to put me in the expert category.

But I wanted to be an expert. I spent many Saturday afternoons at the movies watching Dale Evans riding her horse, Buttermilk, across the silver screen. She had no trouble at all keeping up with Roy. And she never even lost her hat. You've got to admire that.

I wrote her a fan letter one time. It was the only one I ever wrote, and she sent me back a black and white, eight-by-ten picture of her and Buttermilk. The day that came in the mail, I felt like she and I were on a personal, best-friend basis with each other.

And anyone who was a personal, best friend of Dale Evans surely must have some sort of built-in, natural horse-riding ability. So when fair time rolled around the next year, I sat much taller in the merry-go-round saddle. And after that, my natural horsemanship wasn't even in question as far as I was concerned.

That attitude clicked into my subconscious mind so that even after I reached adulthood it was still there—dormant perhaps, but alive and well, nevertheless.

So when I was in my early twenties, I never gave it a second thought when a friend of mine invited several of us to go horseback riding at her ranch. Now, riding a horse doesn't necessarily require expertise if you have friends who know what they are doing and can help you, but it does help if you use a little common sense. Which I didn't.

To begin with, I bought a pair of boots that, as the song says, "were made for walking," not riding. In fact, forget riding, I was having enough trouble just walking in them. It was worse than when I got my first pair of high-heeled shoes.

I have a feeling that even the horse was laughing at me when I walked out to the corral looking as if I had already stepped in something I shouldn't have.

The horses were already saddled and ready to go when we got there. I was given a pretty brown one—I think, in horse circles, it would be called chestnut. Anyhow, she hadn't been ridden since she had her colt, and I was warned that she might be a little rambunctious.

In fact, I was told, it might be better if I rode a more mild-mannered horse.

Now that was an insult to my newly reactivated "expert" attitude.

I assured them that it would be no problem since I was—I had the oddest urge to say a friend of Dale Evans—a pretty good rider. I told them I had ridden horses when I was growing up. I didn't tell them they were hitched to a merry-go-round.

We had been riding for about an hour, and I was feeling like an old hand at this riding thing. However, it did seem a little strange to be riding in a straight line instead of a circle. After a while, the friend whose dad owned the ranch decided to let her horse run.

Now, this girl was raised on a horse. She was probably riding before she was walking. So for her, riding a horse at a full gallop was perfectly natural.

For me, riding a horse at a full gallop was D-U-M-B!! But did I let that stop me? Not at all!

The horse I was riding had been feeling a little antsy anyway, so she was only too happy to oblige my "giddyap" command. Actually, it wasn't a command, it was more of a request because deep down in my heart I knew that I really shouldn't be doing "giddyap." But she "giddyapped," and away we went.

It was wonderful! The wind in my face, the bouncing—and I was definitely a bouncer. I was even a bouncer in my merry-go-round days. Some people never quite master the art of smooth riding, and I was one of them.

We reached a place under a tree, and my friend was quite pleased that I was able to keep up with her—and so was I!

"Would you like to race to the creek bed?" she asked.

I looked back at the rest of the group walking their horses in our direction, and I gave them a condescending smile. Bless their hearts, they were doing very well for beginners.

"Sure! But I need to do something with this stirrup, I'm having a little bit of trouble keeping my foot in it," I replied.

That in itself was a novelty because "keeping my foot in it" had never been the problem before. It was keeping my "foot out of it" that always seemed to give me trouble.

"Don't worry about the stirrups. Wrap your legs around the horse's belly like you're riding bareback. That'll probably work better for you; it does for me," she said, wrapping her own legs around her horse's stomach.

"Hey, that works fine," I replied, ignoring the small, hysterical voice in my head that was yelling as loudly as it could, *ARE YOU OUT OF YOUR MIND!!*

"Well, let's GO!" she said, spurring her horse into a run.

Now, I didn't spur my horse because, for one thing, I wasn't wearing spurs. But also, I was still trying to get comfortable just saying "giddyap."

As it was, I didn't even need to say all of that. I said, "Giddy—," and that was all I had time to say before my horse took off at a dead run. I never knew an animal could go from zero to 110 miles per hour in ten seconds. I'm sure it was faster than the speed of sound, because we left the "giddy—" far behind, just hanging in midair.

That's when I discovered that wrapping your legs around a horse's stomach does work fine—as long as you're standing still.

But when that horse is running so fast that her feet probably aren't even touching the ground, it's not quite the same.

I first realized I was in trouble when I found myself looking straight into that horse's ear. Without the stirrups to keep me in place, I was sliding around and off the horse.

"WHOA!" I yelled, and my "whoa" was much louder than my "giddy—."

But this horse either wasn't listening or just chose to ignore me—I think I was being ignored. If I ever got off that horse, I was going to have to practice putting a little more authority in my "whoa!"

I did manage to get off the horse—head first. I hit the ground bouncing like a rubber ball. When I hit, I heard something that sounded like a tree limb breaking, and it went through my mind that I must have landed in some brush.

As for the horse, she kept right on going. You'd think she would have at least stopped to see if I was all right. I tell you what, I'll take a dog over a horse anytime—they're much more loyal! And right at that moment, I'd have taken a snake over that horse.

But to tell the truth, it wasn't the horse's fault.

Some of the problem had to do with a lack of communication. When I said, "Giddyap," I could hear the merry-go-round music rise to a crescendo, but what the horse heard was the cavalry charge being blown.

As soon as I realized I was lying on the ground, I pushed myself up to a sitting position, only to fall back down. That's when I discovered my wrist looked awfully funny, kind of like a miniature roller coaster track.

I just kept sitting there looking at it. It didn't hurt—yet. Later, it made up for lost time. But I had never seen anything like that, especially on me.

"Are you all right?" my friend yelled as she turned her horse around to come back and survey the damage.

"I think I broke my wrist," I said, still staring at the unnatural angle my wrist had taken.

"This is no time to make jokes!" she yelled again spurring her horse on. "Are you hurt?"

"YES! I THINK I BROKE MY WRIST!!" This time I was doing the yelling. What did I have to say to convince her I had broken my wrist! Actually, maybe I didn't break my wrist. Maybe it was just bent out of shape.

She reigned her horse in.

"Oh, my gosh, your chin!" she said, looking at my skinned face.

Now I had skinned my chin, but it was only a skinned chin. My wrist was really beginning to look weird.

"FORGET MY CHIN!!!" I yelled, and then in a much smaller voice I said, looking down at the odd shape that had once been a pretty good place to keep my watch. "Look at my wrist."

I was hoping she was going to look at it and say, "Oh, I did mine that way one time. It'll get its shape back in an hour or so."

But instead, she said, "OH, MY GOSH!! YOUR WRIST!!!"

So much for getting its shape back.

In the meantime, one of our other friends had managed to catch the horse and bring her back to the crime scene.

"Let me help you back on the horse, and we'll ride to the house and get the car. You've got to go get that wrist set," my friend was saying.

This time, the small still voice in my head made a very vocal outward appearance, "ARE YOU OUT OF YOUR MIND!!" I yelled. "I'm not getting back on that thing!!"

Now my friend was losing patience. I had just referred to her horse as "that thing." That was like calling one of my dogs a cur.

"We're too far from the house for you to walk. How are you going to get back? I can't carry you!"

I looked around, hoping to spot a bus stop conveniently located out in the middle of that horse pasture.

"I don't know," I said, "but I'm not getting back on that horse."

The horse was probably thinking, "That's fine with me. She rides like a sack of potatoes."

There was a big log a few yards away. We decided I would sit down on that and wait for her to ride home and bring the car back for me.

And so ended my horse riding for the time being. And that old adage about needing to get back on a horse as soon as you fall off—whoever said that didn't break something when she took a spill. If she even had a spill—she might have been talking to one of her friends who fell off and broke something. Because I still don't think that friend of mine would have gotten back on her horse if she had broken her wrist. She'd have been the one sitting on a log.

After I mended, I did go back and ride again—it was a different horse, but I didn't ask for a different one. I think maybe the horse made that request when she heard I was coming back. However, when I did get back on a horse, I limited my riding to nothing faster than a trot, and a slow trot at that.

As for filing things away in my subconscious mind, there's one word I tried to file there in capital letters: PRUDENCE! "A prudent man sees danger and takes refuge, but the simple keep going and suffer for it" (Proverbs 22:3).

Under — Way, Way Under — Construction

Do you take this man for better or for worse, for richer or for poorer, and through all phases of construction?" Actually, our wedding vows didn't include that last part, but knowing what I know now, it would have been appropriate.

When Len and I made the decision to build a house while we lived in it, we had no idea what we were getting into.

It was a dream we'd had for a long time, and it took several years to get into position to launch that dream. While I don't regret any of it, I wouldn't want to do it every day. We found that launching that particular dream was like launching the Goodyear Blimp with a kite string.

I can think of many words more pleasant than construction—*root canal, dry rot, bunions, ingrown toenails*—none of these words make me hyperventilate. But let me hear that one dreaded word—*construction*—and it's paper bag time!

It wasn't always that way. When we first started discussing the prospect of building our own house, it seemed exciting and adventurous. We were setting forth into new, unexplored territory for us, not unlike the early pioneers.

Thinking about the early pioneer women working alongside their husbands, helping them carve a home out of the wilderness, always had sort of romantic overtones for me.

But when you really think about it, it wasn't all that romantic. In the first place, I don't think the guys looked that much like Clark Gable or Robert Redford.

This "romantic fantasy" might have held water before photography was invented, but have you ever taken a good look at some of those old photos of early homesteaders? Those people do not look like happy campers.

The men are always very stern-looking, almost glaring at the camera. And the women—they really look bent out of shape. It looks like they're thinking, *If somebody doesn't invent the dishwasher soon, I'm outta here!*

But at the time Len and I decided to build our own house, we weren't thinking about tired-looking folks glaring into a camera that seemed to have interrupted some sort of endurance test. We were thinking about how much money we would save by doing the building ourselves. Besides, we could move into it before it was finished and work on it while we lived there.

It seemed like a good idea at the time, but that's what they said about the Edsel.

When Len was a young man, he worked as a carpenter, so he knows how to build a house, but the trick is building a house with me as a helper and at the same time, holding down a full-time job.

At first, it was like this—he'd come home from work, put on his carpenter's apron, and grab a hammer. He would hit a nail two good whacks—*Bam, Bam*—and it was in solid. I'd hit a nail two good whacks—*bam, bam*—then two more whacks—*bam, bam*—then two more—*bam, bam*—one more—*bam*—and then it was in solid. By then, my arm was tired, and I'd have to rest for five minutes.

So, while I took five, Len would be hammering and whistling. It seemed like a good arrangement to me, and he *is* a good whistler.

The first hint of Len's being a disgruntled worker came when I realized he wasn't whistling anymore. At first, I thought he had switched to singing, but upon listening more closely, I discovered he wasn't singing, he was talking—to the nails.

"Take that, yeah, and that!" he was saying, emphasizing each "that" with a snarl.

So, many, many growls, snarls, and mashed fingers later, we are reaping the benefits and the liabilities of living in a house while we build it.

It *still* isn't completely finished—there will always be something to do, particularly in the plumbing department.

We finally reached a point at which Len needed outside help. But finding someone was quite a job in itself. We called the employment service, and they sent a couple of guys out, which was a big help to Len.

It was especially helpful right at that time, because I had to have a foot surgery. For a while, he had to do without my assistance, regardless of how little it was. Actually, losing me as a helper was the best thing that happened because the guys that replaced me . . . that's right, I said *guys*—it took more than one to replace me, even if I did have to take a five minute break after each nail—anyhow, they got a lot done, and it made Len realize how nice it was to have some regular help.

But in all fairness to me, maybe they did get more done, but they didn't have to stop to cook supper and run the kids to Little League, and so forth.

If someone had taken my picture during the time I was helping with the building, I'd have looked a lot like certain pictures I've seen of pioneer women.

So, when I decided to have my foot surgery done—a heel spur that had to be removed—I was kind of glad for the break. But after the surgery, it didn't take me long to decide I'd rather be hammering nails.

At the point I had the foot surgery, we had sheet-rocked the bathroom connected to our bedroom, but we hadn't textured the walls. So if you looked up at the ceiling in our bathroom, you could see the upstairs area through the cracks where the sheet rock didn't quite meet, and vice versa. But we didn't really have to worry about the vice versa because we had temporarily closed the upstairs area until we finished the downstairs.

We didn't even have a staircase yet. Len just used a ladder when he needed to go up there to wire things or whatever he was doing at the time.

On this particular day, he had the three men from the employment agency out there to help him. They were working outside putting siding on the house.

My doctor had finally given me permission to take a shower. I still couldn't put any weight on my foot, and I was using crutches part of the time and a wheelchair part of the time.

Of course, there was no way I could get the wheelchair into the shower, so I had tried to get in there with the crutches, but it was too slick.

I had decided I would have to forgo the pleasure of a good hot shower and content myself with just looking forward to one, when I got a fabulous idea.

Len was outside working with the carpenters, so I hobbled out to the back porch and got a lightweight, aluminum lawn chair. Len would be surprised when he came in and discovered how inventive I had been without even having asked his help.

Our shower was a small, temporary plastic job that didn't have a top. It was basically just an enclosure with a shower head in it. Len had put it in to use until we got the permanent one in there.

I put the chair in the shower and adjusted the water to a delicious, very warm temperature. I couldn't wait to get in. I hadn't been able to shower since my surgery.

At first, I felt a little ridiculous sitting in a lawn chair in my shower in the altogether. But I was enjoying that shower so much that soon I wasn't even thinking about how silly it must look. Besides, who was going to see me?

The sun shining through the upstairs window found the cracks in the bathroom ceiling and shone down in cheerful little beams into the shower. All in all, it was very relaxing. I couldn't remember enjoying anything that much in a long time.

Suddenly, the sunbeams were interrupted by a shadow. A shadow?

Now what could cause that? I looked up and saw one of the carpenters walking around upstairs above my shower! Len, not knowing what I was doing, had sent one of them up there to get something.

It had taken me several minutes to get situated in that shower when I first got in, but getting out was much, much quicker! I couldn't have gotten out of that shower any quicker if Norman Bates' mother had been after me!

Needless to say, I kept a low profile until the carpenters left. After they went home, Len came in, and I pounced.

"What was that carpenter doing upstairs, and why didn't you tell me he was going up there?"

"He was getting some more siding and nails. Why did you need to know that?"

"Because I was taking a shower sitting in the lawn chair, that's why!"

"You were taking a shower in the lawn chair?" he asked, looking at me as though I had finally lost it.

"Yes, and it was working fine until 'company' dropped in," I said.

"Well, he didn't act like he had seen anything unusual when he came back. He probably didn't notice," he said.

What more was there to say? Not much. But I made myself scarce every time he came back after that.

Building our house was an experience for us, and it took us a little longer than we planned because we stopped many times with our kids, to smell the roses along the way. Now we have our house—and a nose full of thorns—but no regrets.

I'm just glad somebody invented those little sticky tabs to put on the wall for hanging pictures. Otherwise, my walls would be bare, because I never want to whack another nail!

I'm also glad we're not going to have to build our own house in heaven. The Master Carpenter will have it ready and waiting for us when we get there. We won't have to so much as lift a hammer! The construction will be finished. I really like that part. Besides, I happen to know that the Lord is a much better plumber than we are.

"Now we know that if the earthly tent we live in is destroyed, we have a building from God, an eternal house in heaven, not built by human hands" (2 Corinthians 5:1).